MODERN DAY CHRISTIAN MYSTICS

A COMPILIATION OF MYSTICAL REVELATIONS AND ENCOUNTERS

MODERN DAY CHRISTIAN MYSTICS

ISBN-13: 978-0692243510
ISBN-10: 0692243518

Edited by Stefanie Overstreet, Hailley Jo Holcombe
Written and compiled by Denise Allen, Lauren Detombe, Kalina Georgieva,
Tim Oliver, Daniel Ruggaber, Nick Wallace, and a myriad of mystics.
Illustrations by Daniel Ruggaber, Nick Wallace
Website Design by Nick Wallace
Team Leader Nick Wallace
Printed in the United States of America.
First printing, 2014

This book is a work of non-fiction. Names, places, and incidents are not fabricated
but actual recorded incidents of history or testimonies from specified individuals.
Revelations and encounters recorded in this book involve individuals who are self-
proclaimed mystics, as defined by this work.

BOOK WEBSITE

To view content and additional interviews, download a QR Code Reader and scan the QR codes placed throughout the book.

TRY ME

If a QR Code Reader is not available, all interviews and content may also be found at the website below:

http://moderndaymystics.wix.com/christianmystics

BOOK ICONS

Throughout the book, there are several icons placed at the top of the page. These icons will help you identify whether the mystic or information you are reading is "Biblical" or "Historical." The "Biblical" and "Historical" concepts are meant to illustrate that we serve a God who does not change and has always intended to personally interact with humanity.

Historical

Biblical

SCHOLARSHIP FUND

One hundred percent of this book's proceeds will create a scholarship fund for current and future ministry school students needing tuition aide.

Through this fund we will provide resources for students wanting to transform the world through the knowledge that God is good, that He is still speaking, and that His presence and love is enough to restore the most hardened hearts and regions. Revival is a product of connecting to His heart, saying what He is saying, and do what He is doing.

As we enjoy Him we become like Him, this is the intent of mysticism.

ACKNOWLEDGEMENTS

Mystics – thank you for expressing a nature of God that many tend to shy away from, for making the pursuit of God your daily bread, and for continually enlarging our understanding of how God meets with mankind.

Anne Kalvestrand – thank you for your fearless pursuit of God. You break the mold and redefine what a modern day revivalist looks like, and you have utterly smashed our traditional concept of how one might serve the Lord.

Bethel School of Supernatural Ministry – thank you for training up a generation of sold-out lovers of God, for equipping the Saints for the work of the Lord, and for inspiring us all to reach a little higher by looking for Heaven's model to transform earth.

CONTENTS

FOREWORD

Anne M. Kalvestrand // *Director, The Art of Peace Institute*

All of history has waited for a company of people created for God's praise. In this book, the reader will step into the abundant lives of individuals who have pursued God and listened to Him. The accounts shared in this book show the reader what it looks like to enjoy a rich history of faithfulness with the Lord. The people that were interviewed made themselves still and listened to the Lord. They have quieted their souls and beheld the Lord.

Nick and his team conducted interviews with individuals who have pursued the presence of God. In this book, these individuals have shared their quest of pursuing the Lord, and their stories demonstrate the Lord's response to such hunger.

In essence, this book shows the reader how to love God well. In the process, the reader will see the Lord high and lifted up. They will meet the Lord and see Him as the Lion of the Tribe of Judah. They will see Him as the Lamb who was slain before the foundations of the world for you and for me. The reader will walk in the cool of the day with the Lord as they read accounts of what happens when one spends time with God.

In this book, the reader gets to see the Lord in all His glory as revealed by His friends. The Old Testament prophet Jeremiah said that if we were to ask, the Lord would show us great and mighty things that we did not know.

These are not things that can be obtained through hard work. Jeremiah saw the things to come that we are able to enjoy today. This book contains many answers to the Lord's promise through the prophet Jeremiah.

One key difference between Christianity and other world religions is that we are to enjoy God as a friend. The accounts revealed in this book are from people who have walked in the cool of the day with the Lord and enjoyed His friendship. The individuals who were interviewed were able to balance walking in the fear of the Lord and delighting in His pleasure as His pure, glorious bride. The conversations and interactions they had with the Lord are shared so that we all will love the Lord more.

The Jewish sages believed that day began at dusk. Between dusk and morning, the Lord would create all night long. When God's people woke up, they stepped into all the Lord had prepared for them all night long. The Lord is a Creator, and His people are able to enjoy all that He created for them. This book provides an account of what the Lord has prepared for us and for the nations in this hour. It equips the reader to step into the richness of the Lord's provision for His people.

As you read, remember that the Lord has journeys and adventures that He wants to go on with you. The Lord desires that His original intent of walking with Him in the cool of the day would be restored. This is one of those rare books that cause the reader to love God more and know Him better.

THE PURPOSE

Nick Wallace // MDCM Anthology Team // United States

Introduction

It was about 3:00 a.m. on November 14th, 2010. In the dream, an apostle was standing before a great multitude declaring, "A nation is not established on the words of a *king* but on the words of the *LORD*!" Chills ran through every part of my being as this chant, like marching orders, pulsated within me. As if a declaration of war was being laid forth, confidently the Body of Christ rose up under these commands—no longer worrying about who had earthly authority because they knew with great assurance that God's Word would prevail. When I awoke, the emotions of the dream were still alive. As if implanted in me, they only had one aim left—to be recreated.

Teachings and sermons are extremely necessary, but there is something distinctive that a personal encounter implants in you that is unlike anything else. It brings breath to what we read and makes words into an actual experience with memories and emotions tied to them. My encounter sparked a thirst inside much different from anything I had experienced before. It brought life to the pages of the Bible for me, making them a clear and present day reality. I would never say that an individual must have encounters to be close to God, but I would say, it certainly helps.

God is the same today as He was yesterday, never to change. If He was speaking in Biblical times, then He is speaking now. If He spoke through dreams then, He will also now. Too many times we read the encounters of those in the Bible as mere stories instead of models of a relationship God has for us today. The aim of "Modern Day Christian Mystics" is exactly that. In this book you, will read many stories from individuals that have encountered God in the same ways as those in Biblical times. This includes everything from dreams, visions of Jesus, transportations, heavenly encounters, etc. This book will most certainly stretch your expectation for how God desires to interact with His body.

To illustrate this interaction, we found and interviewed individuals that encounter God like the saints of old. In this book, we refer to those interviewed as "mystics," which is further defined in the following chapter. Also scattered throughout the book are Biblical and Historical stories that resemble the ones of those interviewed. We did this to further illustrate the similarity of how God interacts with His followers all throughout history and the Bible.

Interpretation

The revelations and encounters recorded in this book must always be viewed through the context of scripture. Our intention is not to tell you how to think or get you to believe everything you read. We want you to use your mind, Holy Spirit, and test the revelations and encounters against Scripture.

The Point Of It All

More than anything, we want the reader to learn that we serve a tangible God that intends to be grasped and interacted with. We hope these encounters and the lifestyle of the mystics interviewed will create a hunger in you for greater union with God. We hope that as you read the book, the encounters would leap from the pages and ignite your hearts for the sake of Christ and His purpose—reviving our heart to love.

The point of it all is to become more like Christ. By definition, Jesus was the greatest mystic to ever walk the earth. He lived a life completely unified and in sync with His Father. There was no separation between His will and His Father's will (John 5:19). There was never any confusion about what God was saying which gave Him a perfect ear to the Father's heart. He was able to discern the voice of the Lord in any situation and therefore bring Heaven to Earth at any time. Mysticism is about connecting to His heart alone and communicating what He says, no matter what the situation looks like, knowing in the end His word will always prevail. And as we encounter Him, how can we not become more like Him? This is the intent of mysticism!

John 15: 4 – 5 *"4 Remain in me, as I also remain in you. No branch can bear fruit by itself; it must remain in the vine. Neither can you bear fruit unless you remain in me. 5 "I am the vine; you are the branches. If you remain in me and I in you, you will bear much fruit; apart from me you can do nothing."*

CHAPTER ONE

Denise Allen // MDCM Anthology Team // Jamaica

"Mysticism is the art of union with Reality. The mystic is a person who has attained that union in greater or less degree; or who aims at and believes in such attainment."

Evelyn Underhill (a well-known 20th century English mystic)

Defining Mysticism

Mystics and the practice of mysticism are not exclusive to just one faith or religion, but they can be found in many faiths around the world. For the sake of clarity, we believe union with God is only possible through the Holy Spirit and belief in Jesus as Lord and Savior. The mystics addressed in this book hold the same belief.

The word 'mystic' is derived from a Greek word *mystikos,* which refers to someone who shuts their eyes in order to shut out the mundane world and experience other realities.   The Oxford Dictionary defines mysticism as, "the belief, that union with or absorption into the Deity or the absolute, or the spiritual apprehension of knowledge inaccessible to the intellect, may be attained through contemplation and self-surrender."

Attributes of Christian Mystics

Mysticism in Christianity has existed since the founding fathers of the faith. According to Bernard McGinn, a renown scholar on Christian mystics, the term "mystical" has been widely used by Christians since the second century CE to refer to "secret realities of their beliefs, rituals, and practices, especially to the mystical meaning of the Bible, that is the inner message of God that may be found beneath the literal sense of the scriptural text and stories[2]." At the core of Christian mysticism is inner transformation. The authenticity of a mystic is measured not only by his or her transformation, but also the transformation of those whom the mystic affects.

Beni Johnson's *The Happy Intercessor* describes Christian mystics as "people who have laid down their entire lives to seek after one thing, the very heart of God. One of the things that make 'mystics' different from other people is that they have only one desire, to know God in His fullness."

There are a number of factors that characterize Christian mystics. The first is that mysticism is not acquired by the individual but is a gift from God. It is a calling, which may start from early childhood, such as with Joan of Arc, or much later in life as with the Apostle Paul. Mystics recognize this call and completely surrender themselves to God. Underhill puts it this way, "The training mystics undergo of renunciation of self opens them to both deep and wide, embracing in its span all those aspects of Reality (God)."

Beni Johnson writes, "Mystics are people who live in a right relationship with God and who have truly surrendered themselves to knowing Him more, no matter the cost... mystics are people who have a continuous awareness of God... mystics see beyond this reality and into the spirit realm... to them God is more real than life. God is their life... they see how Heaven invades earth... mystics are able to see into the spiritual realm and use it to define what is in the earthly realm... to the mystic the spirit realm is a safe place. To them, the spiritual realm can often seem more real than the earthly realm[3]."

Christian mysticism is more than an encounter, a moment or brief state of mystical union; it is an ongoing process of communion with a God. The Apostle Paul's statement in Philippians 3:10-11 NIV persuasively expresses this desire for an ongoing communion with God, "I want to know Christ and the power of his resurrection and the fellowship of sharing in His suffering, becoming like Him in death, and so, somehow, to attain the resurrection from the dead."

McGinn argues that a proper grasp of mysticism requires an investigation of the ways by which mystics have prepared for God's intervention in their lives and the affect that divine action has had upon the mystic and those to whom she or he has communicated the message. There are a various descriptions of "preparation" that McGinn refers to. For example, many scholars of mysticism suggest a pathway from awakening to purgation, illumination and union. More simply, Underhill developed a five-stage framework whereby the individual ultimately enters into union with God. Yet these frameworks should not be confining since the grace of God is highly unpredictable. God's plan for each person is unique to that person.

Who Are Christian Mystics

Over the ages, Christian mystics have approached their unique relationship with God in a variety of ways, often influenced by the religious practices and beliefs of their time. What stands out in the accounts of Christian mystics is that their encounters with God transform them completely, and they are compelled to share the things they learn through their encounters.

We often associate mystics with well-known personalities of the past such as Augustine, John of the Cross, Catherine of Genoa, Joan of Arc, St.

Francis of Assisi, most of which are from the Catholic faith. Consequently there is a common belief that mystics are rare and even relegated to the past. Yet as Underhill pointed out, "If the Church continues to be a living and enduring fact, a true organism, the mystical element of her corporate life must endure, and bring from time to time its gift supernatural joy and certitude, since it arises in the soul's experience of the community as a whole."

No one really knows how many mystics there are in the world, yet in every period of the Christian church, the numbers of hidden mystics most assuredly exceed those recorded. They are drawn from all walks of life and vocations. Some are famous scientists like Isaac Newton, the father of modern science. Others remain unknown like Lucie-Christine, a French woman, housewife and mother of five children whose journals revealing her mystical journey were discovered after her death. Here's an excerpt from her diary of her encounter with God: "My soul found itself transported into the Infinity of God; not merely as into some new region, but as if, having lost it's own life, it was living in the Infinite itself.[1]"

These unknown and known Christian mystics are life-giving members of the Church, and they bring to life the rich history of God interacting with humankind. The ensuing stories of the Modern Mystics interviewed depict the same pursuit of God as the historical and Biblical mystics. Outside of cultural variance, you will find that many of their stories reflect and emulate the Biblical stories we've grown up with while holding fast to the same truths. God is still calling His people to action, but will we have ears to hear and eyes to see? Or will we miss His message because of the way it's delivered?

1   Evelyn Underhill, '*Practical Mysticism - A little book for normal people*,' E.P. Dutton &Co. 1915, released June 8, 2007.
2   Bernard McGinn, 'The essential writings of Christian Mysticism,' The Modern Library 2006.
3   Beni Johnson, '*The Happy Intercessor,*' Destiny Image Publishers 2009.
4   Evelyn Underhill, '*Mystics of the Church*,' Morehouse Publishing

CHAPTER TWO

Interviews

Angels
Dance
Dreams
Heaven
Miracles
Other
The Process
Transportations
Visions

ANGELS

ANGELS, DREAMS, AND THE SUPERNATURAL
Steve Moore // Mystic // United States

While I was in college I began praying for people on the streets and started to see people get healed. I began talking to God, asking Him: what is possible? What do we have access to, and how can we experience You more? One night I just felt a sense before I went to bed to pray and give God the opportunity to encounter me in the night.

While sleeping I had a dream so real that I felt like I was there. I was separated from my body, and I could see myself lying on a round porch high up in the air with a stone-wall and double doors on one side, while the other side was open. Then an angel came and said, "Wake up child for now is the time to sound the alarm for the glory of the Lord." When he spoke I felt a cold rushing wind or liquid sensation go from my head down my spine. In the dream, I woke up and ran through the doors that were in the wall.

When I awoke I heard a horn with my physical ears, almost like a Shofar or another big loud horn. Then I looked over at my phone, and I saw a text message from a friend at 4:00 a.m. The text had the passage Romans 10:13-15, "How can they be saved unless someone preaches, how can they hear the good news unless someone is sent, how beautiful are the feet of those who spread the good news." When I read it, the Lord spoke to me and said, "Look at your feet." So I pulled back the sheets and my feet were covered with actual dirt and mud. This was not in the spirit but physical mud.

All of a sudden the Presence of God came in the room, and I began to be encountered by His love and goodness. He started speaking to me about proclaiming who He is and letting people know what they have access to in

Him and His goodness. This lasted for about an hour. Then right before I went back to sleep, I asked God to confirm what just happened.

Later that morning when I woke up, I got into the shower and looked down to see that the water was dirty and muddy. I was not imagining the dirt on my feet last night. My roommate sent me another text and told me that he thought I should look into Ezekiel 33. When I read it, it talked about how Ezekiel was a watchman. He was supposed to warn the people about the coming glory of the Lord. God started to speak to me about how now is the time and age where His Spirit is permeating throughout the whole world. We have the opportunity and access to experience it in different realms and areas—more than ever before. He was also impressing on me to speak about the uniqueness and goodness of God. From that point, He took me on a journey of intentional dreaming about the access we have in Him. I went through this amazing season where He spoke to me in new ways and encounters as I slept. It was like I was actually experiencing Him and my body could feel the dreams and His presence.

When I came to school at BSSM, I was with three friends in my bedroom telling testimonies about how God is so good, encounters with angels, and weird manifestations of glory. All of a sudden this feather about an inch and a half long appears and began floating around us. Then the presence of God fell in the room, and all these feathers started appearing in the air. It was the weirdest experience, but in the matter of about 10 minutes there was about 100 feathers swirling in our room. Not just floating, but actually swirling in our room like a whirlpool. The Presence of God was thick.

One my friends said, "I feel like we are supposed to invite angels in the room." When we said, "Angels, we give you permission to enter our room," our bedroom door slowly began to open and the door handle slowly began to move up. As soon as the door opened, we all felt the exact same thing I encountered from the angel in my dream, a cold rushing wind and liquid sensation shooting up and down our spines. The door swung open by itself; nobody was around and nobody was touching it. But this new shift came into the room… a physical presence like we had never felt before.

At this point we started getting rocked by the Presence of God. It was a weird feeling. It felt like my body was being pressed by weight but at the same time it felt light and peaceful. It felt like I was moving my whole body through mud—it was just so thick. My friend John pointed and told me there was an angel behind me. When I turned and reached up my hand in the air, electricity started shooting through my fingertips and went up my arm. I decided not to tell them what was happening. Then they all came over to stick their arms where mine was, and they all started freaking out saying, "It's like electricity!" For the next four hours we felt electricity permeating our bodies, the Presence of God, the feathers swirled the entire time and angels kept encountering us.

God started to speak to us, "If you'll have Me, I'll establish My glory here in a tangible way in the house." Then He shared about how all throughout scripture it says that we have the Godhead in us, the fullness in us. So we started praying and ushering in His Presence. When the Presence fell, I got filled and drunk on the Spirit like I've never been before—where I couldn't even lift my head. It felt heavy like a cinder block. We were just worshipping like that for the next two hours. After that night, there was a tangible smell, like vanilla, that permeated the room from that point on.

In the Bible, God's weighty manifest Presence would rest on particular places or people, so we decided: why not our room? From that point on it became our "encounter room." We hooked up an iPod to speakers to play worship music all day and night. For eight months that room smelled like vanilla, not like a vanilla scent that you would spray, but like a sweet aroma. This tangible Presence in the room would be there whenever we wanted an encounter. We would just lay down and encounter God, whether it was by a vision, dream or increased Presence. Feathers would manifest, and glory dust would form on our hands and face. It opened up our paradigm of what was actually possible and what we can actually steward and possess.

That experience really impressed upon me that it's not enough to preach the gospel. Jesus dying for us so that we could have forgiveness of sins is just the access point but once inside the door, there is so much more to this Christian life than we think. We have full access to Heaven and Himself! He started speaking to me saying, "Steve, if you think the spiritual experiences that witch doctors have are just reserved for them, you are severely mistaken. Those are just manipulations, a counterfeit, of what I have for My Body."

This opened the realm of God as being the God of the impossible and encounters. I went on a journey of encountering Him in ways like never before. There is story after story that I could tell about the manifest Presence and glory of God showing up. Being able to tell the testimony and actually see other people experience it has been life changing for me. These encounters are not just for my friends and me. There is actually an invitation to impart encounters to everyone who receives Jesus as Lord and Savior.

Listen to Audio

GOD WANTS US TO SEE
Dawn Oleary // Mystic // Canada

In 2008, I went to Israel. While I was at Mt Carmel (the mountain where Elijah called down fire), I closed my eyes and the Lord spoke to me in a vision. I saw Jesus on the cross with thorns around His head and nails in His hands, and I heard Him clearly speak to me. He simply said: "If this had just been for you, I still would have gone to the cross." He has the same sentiment for everybody.

To me, seeing angels all around is natural. You don't need to have a specific gift. Basically I know that God loves me so much, therefore He lets me see. This is a gift that anybody can have. You just need to let Him love you. That is how encounters happen—just say, "God, I love you so much," and encounters will flow from this. God wants to show us His Kingdom simply because He loves us so much. If we want it, we can have it. I think sometimes we make spiritual matters harder than they actually need to be. When we let Him completely love us, we will see more things in the spirit.

"To me, seeing angels all around is natural."

A lot of people have the ability to see but don't realize it because they think it has to "look" a certain way. A lot of people have supernatural encounters but don't realize it. For example, have you ever woken up in the morning and you're singing a particular song? I think this sometimes happens because angels have been signing this song over us during the night. Remember, supernatural encounters will not necessarily look like you think they will look. I want all people to understand just how much they are desperately loved by God. I can feel His heart for people. He does not see our flaws; He just loves us!

ANGELS EVERYWHERE
Jason Smedley // Mystic // United States

There was a season in my life where I physically saw angels flying around the sky all the time. I see angels everywhere now, but at the time, it was specifically always high up in the sky. At times I would see one dart from one side of the horizon to the other in the blink of an eye, but it was following a scattered pattern similar to a lightning bolt! Other times they would appear and disappear then reappear again. The angels had what looked like battle formations. Once while I was leading a team of missionaries in Cambodia, a giant 50 foot tall angel (at least), flew through the air in the direction of Thailand, showing me to head to Thailand. In much the same way, the star led the Magi towards Jesus as He lay in the manger.

Angels were showing up in the sky all the time, to be seen physically, not just in the spirit. On one occasion, I was helping serve a ministry in Los Angeles, CA with a friend. I looked up in the sky and saw around 8 or 9 angels flying in formation towards the north. They were glowing with brilliant white light. Honestly, as anyone with this kind of gifting will know, I began to question my sanity. So I thought up a brilliant plan! If my friend could see the angels too, then I would know I wasn't crazy!

So I ran over to my friend Stephen and said, "Stephen, there are angels in the air, and I want you to come see them!" He ran outside with me, and we both stopped and looked up into the sky. I still saw them, but he just looked and kept blinking. "Do you see them?!" I excitedly asked. "No," he responded. That settled it; I was crazy! In a last ditch effort I asked him to look again, more intently this time. Just as I was giving up on him being able to see these angels, he suddenly gasped loudly, "Oh my! There they are! I see them!" When he said, "I see them!" my eyes were opened up to an even greater degree. Suddenly I saw around 12 more angels appear in the sky all around the white colored ones, except these ones were radiating with blue light all around them! Astonished I said, "Blue angels! Can you see them?!" But no matter how hard he looked, all he saw were the white ones.

The Lord spoke to me through this situation. He said to me that as I allow people to step into what I can see, He will open up my gifting to a whole new level and allow me to see even more! This is why I train people in the prophetic and seer realms of revelation. Give and you shall receive! I have made a commitment in my life to hold back none of my prophetic "secrets" but to share them all. Because in so doing the Lord has given me a promise that He will give me a double portion. I have had highly gifted seers tell me that I can teach people to prophesy, but not to see in the spirit. Sometimes people say this because their gifting has become their identity. If everybody can do it, then they feel they will lose their elevated status that they cling to so dearly in order to feel valuable and important.

I don't blame them; I've had those feelings too. But I have committed my life to utterly abandon my sense of self-preservation and share everything that the Lord has taught and showed me about operating in revelation. This is because an army is being raised up on the earth that will operate in signs and wonders and realms of revelation unheard of by any generation that has ever come before us! Now is the time for men and women to shatter the platforms they've built for themselves by withholding the secrets of their anointing! Now is the time for the church to become the world's authoritative voice on all things spiritual, mystical and supernatural! The Lord once sent an angel to teach me that those who carry more weight in the spirit will lower themselves. This is because that which is heavy has greater gravitational pull and always goes low. Let us be humble; let us go low.

Joan of Arc
(ca. 1412 - 31)

"Act, and God will act."

"One life is all we have and we live it as we believe in living it. But to sacrifice what you are and to live without belief, that is a fate more terrible than dying."

"I would rather die than do something which I know to be a sin, or to be against God's will."

Daughter of a poor family in a small village in northeastern France, Joan would seem an unlikely candidate for the grandeur of God's call on her life. As a child she had many encounters with angels, and Saints of old, including St. Michael, St. Catherine and St. Margaret. By the age of 13 she began hearing "the voice" of God, which was most always accompanied by a light[1]. "At first the voices simply told her to be good, but eventually they outlined three missions she must undertake: to save Orleans, to enable Charles VII to be officially crowned King of France at Reims Cathedral, and to drive the English out of the country[2]."

By the age of 16 she delivered her first message to a king and showed him a sign that would prove she was from God. Shortly after, she began leading soldiers into battle with much success. Many times before battle she would have visitations that gave her military strategies and details about the battle to lead them to victory. Military commanders recognized that her poise and military knowledge far exceeded even the learned and experienced French captains of her day. She was only 17 years of age.

All three missions given to her by angels were completed before her capture in May 1430. A year later she was charged for wearing men's clothing and heresy, due to her refusal to recant the voices she heard. On May 30th, 1431 she was burned at the stake at just 19 years of age. Though she died at a young age, she lives on in history. "Nearly five centuries after her death, in 1920, she was formally canonized by Pope Benedict XV" as a saint[2]."

1   Steven Butler, *Mystics of the Christian Tradition,* London and New York, Routledge, 2001, p.117 - 118
2   Jon Heggie, *Exploring History*, National Geographics Society, 2011, p. 60, 67

Angels in the Bible

Hebrews 1:14 *"Are they not all ministering spirits, sent out to render service for the sake of those who will inherit salvation?"*

Psalms 91:11 *"For He will give His angels charge concerning you, To guard you in all your ways."*

Angels are mentioned 196 times in the Bible (NASB). They have served many purposes of God, as messengers of judgment, to shut the mouths of lions, or deliver "good tidings of great joy" (Luke 2:10). In the end, we have many Biblical examples to help us best understand the purposes of angels, yet there is no concrete definition that specifically defines their exact function.

The Bible leaves a bit of ambiguity on the subject with some details assumedly thrown in as if we should know, such as humanity judging the angels (1 Cor. 6:3). Whichever way you define their purpose, we do know angels are used in the old and new covenant, and in the End Times. So why wouldn't they have a purpose now?

Here are a couple examples of their uses in the Bible:

Two appear to Lot and tell him to leave Sodom	-Genesis 19
Shut the mouths of lions to protect Daniel	-Daniel 6:22
Broke Peter out of jail	-Acts 12:7
Michael disputes with Satan over Moses' body	-Jude 1:9
Seven letters for the seven Angels of the churches	-Revelations 2-3

The most astonishing angel visitation was when Jesus went into the wilderness for forty days to be tempted by the devil. After He refuted the devil "angels came and began to minister to Him (Matthew 4:11)." So I'll leave you with this thought—if the Son of God needs them, then why wouldn't we?

DANCE

DANCE WITH ME
Saara Taina // Mystic // Finland

I grew up as a gymnast, and I was used to movement, but I had never used it as a part of my spiritual expression. I had just left Finland's national gymnast team and moved to Norway to undertake discipleship training school. It was here that I felt like God was telling me to start using my whole body as an instrument of worship. I had received many prophecies about this since I was very young, but I had never really understood what it meant, as I was a gymnast and never a dancer.

One day, I went into my bedroom and put on some worship music. I invited the Holy Spirit to come and start teaching me how to dance. I told Him that I did not know what to do, but He said that He would teach me if I would let Him show me. And He really did teach me!

It was an experience that is hard to describe with words. One thing I can compare it with is the experience of beginning to speak in tongues. It was like God gave me another language. I began dancing and moving in ways I had neither learned in any class, nor seen anybody else do before. It was as if I received a heavenly language as the Holy Spirit taught me how to express my heart.

I felt that I was able to express emotions that were on my heart which I did not have words for. As I did this, I could feel the presence of the Holy Spirit. It was an incredible feeling, and I felt like my relationship with the Lord had gone to a whole new level. While I still use words when I pray, for me dancing has become another prayer language. I am able to connect with the Holy Spirit in ways that I could not otherwise connect.

Since that initial encounter, God has taken me on a journey to show me how dance is such a powerful weapon in the Kingdom. We can literally "take the land" and release His presence through dance and movement. It is not the dance in itself that is so powerful, but it is His presence on us as we dance and move.

My life message is that Jesus deserves a bride that is free to express everything that she is without any fear or shame. I feel like now is the time that God is releasing everyone to start expressing their worship in new ways. The enemy has stolen a lot of dance and movement for himself because he knows the power that is has. But I feel like God is restoring dance and movement back to the original purpose that it was created for.

As I travel, it has been amazing to see that God is restoring dance all over the world. Also dance is not just for girls—many guys are learning and growing in dance and movement. One scripture that I really feel is for this season is Jeremiah 31:13: "Then young women will dance and be glad, young men and old as well. I will turn their mourning into gladness; I will give them comfort and joy instead of sorrow." Jeremiah 31:3 also talks about the Lord loving us with an everlasting love and drawing us to Himself with loving-kindness. Through dance we can really encounter God's everlasting love.

I feel God is drawing us near with His love, and we are going to be so full of His love that we cannot hold it in. It is going to come out in many creative ways, one of which is dance. I believe that every individual, and also every people group, has something unique to give to God in the area of dance and expressing their hearts to Him in worship through movement. This is because an individual's dance is something that nobody else can give to God. Only you can give to God your individual form of dance and movement.

Watch Saara Taina Interview by Destiny Image
http://www.youtube.com/watch?v=3CQr2Gj0Uws

TEACH ME TO DANCE
AJ // Mystic // United States

My most profound encounter happened when I was with my youth group during a prayer fast leading up to an event we were having. While I was praying, God showed me a picture up in heaven. Usually when I have these encounters it's not like I am actually there, but it is more like a picture or movie screen image that appears in my head.

The picture was of an open field with a large tree in it. It was the typical kids' drawing of a tree with a strong trunk and bushy top. The top of the tree was cut off and there was a lake within the branches, almost like a birdbath. Then the scene changed where Jesus and I were standing in the middle of this lake and He told me that He wanted to show me what I look like in Heaven. In my head, I was thinking that I've already been shown in other encounters what my spirit man looks like so I began to tell Him that. But He said that He wants to show me a part of myself that I've never seen before.

In the picture, I was shirtless with a robe on—almost like a skirt-robe that was from my waist down, and I was a dancer. So I told Him, "That's great God, but I don't dance." I'll come back to this in a minute. Next, among many other visions, He took a diamond and pressed it into my chest. After all this happened, I was a little confused because I didn't know if everything I saw was real or if I was just imagining things.

Either way, as the night continued, our group started praying for one another. God asked me to pray for my spiritual father, Caleb, and do for him what He had just done to me. So as a prophetic act, I took the diamond that Jesus gave me and I put it into his chest. At the end of the prayer meeting, they asked if there is anything people wanted to share. My friend

Hannah began to tell about all the experiences that she'd had during the prayer time. Just as she was about to end she said, "Oh, one more thing. I also saw AJ put a diamond in Caleb's chest!" This was just the confirmation I needed. It made it clear to me that what I had experienced was so real.

"The Holy Spirit actually taught me how to dance! I had never taken a dance lesson in my life."

The next week was the very first time that I ever danced. If you remember my first encounter, God told me that He wanted me to dance. The only problem was that I didn't know how. When I told God this, He responded, "Just do what makes sense." I told Him, "I still don't know how to do that." He then told me that He would lead me, and I just needed to follow. The Holy Spirit actually taught me how to dance! I had never taken a dance lesson in my life. He literally taught me in my prayer time with Him. All I had to do was just follow His lead. Now I dance all the time, which is one of the main ways I encounter Him. If I had never believed the vision He showed me, then I would have missed out on a piece of my identity that was meant for me.

To see AJ dance check out the video under the next interview, 'Mystical Dance'

MYSTICAL DANCE
Church Dance Team

Connection with God develops as we become the individuals He made us to be, as we no longer deny the passions within us and as we respond to how He has made us to connect. One might spend hours in prayer and another might paint. As long as their hearts are postured to the Lord, both equally qualify as worship and connection to God.

In this video, Saara Taina leads a team of mystics in worship as they connect with God through dance.

Watch Dance Video

St. Vitus
(ca. 290 – 303)

St. Vitus was born in Sicily around 290 (exact year unknown) and raised as the only son of a Sicilian Senator. According to legend, Vitus was given to nurse Crescentia and her husband Modestus for education. During this time one of the most intense persecutions in the early Christian church was taking place. But even in the midst of persecution, the nurse raised Vitus in the Christian faith. As soon as his biological father noticed that Vitus didn't worship the Roman gods he did everything he could to convince him to lose his faith in Christ. When all his efforts failed he had his son and his son's tutors tortured and arrested.

One time while his father was visiting him in jail, his father peeked through the keyhole to find his son dancing with seven beautiful angels. From that point on his father was terrified of Vitus. Later Vitus and his tutors were released, and all of them fled to the South where Vitus performed all kinds of miracles and brought glory to God. God provided for them wherever they went, even using an eagle to bring them bread.

When the Roman Emperor Diocletian heard about all the signs and wonders that Vitus was performing, he sent his servants to find him because the Emperor's son was possessed with a number of evil spirits. When the son of the Emperor was healed, Diocletian insisted that Vitus worship the Roman gods and deny the Christian faith[1].

When Vitus did not deny his God the Emperor had him thrown into the arena to be eaten by lions. Instead of killing Vitus, the lions bowed before him and licked his feet. After that Vitus and his tutors were tortured and dipped in hot oils[3]. After they were pulled from the oil, an angel appeared and took all three of them to a different location. Shortly after they died from the wounds inflicted during their torture[2].

Saint Vitus became one of the Patrons of the Catholic Church. In the late Middle-Ages, people in Germany celebrated the Feast of Vitus by dancing around his sculpture[2]. Vitus is known as one of the Fourteen Holy Helpers of the Roman Catholic Church and as the patron saint of dancers and entertainers.

1   https://www.catholic.org/saints/saint.php?saint_id=140
2   http://en.wikipedia.org/wiki/Vitus
3   http://www.catholic-saints.info/patron-saints/saint-vitus.htm

King David
(bc. 1040 – 970)

King David is the only man in the Bible about whom God says, "I have found David the son of Jesse, a man after my own heart, who will do all My will (Acts 13:22)." David cried out, "My soul yearns, even faints, for the courts of the Lord; my heart and my flesh cry out for the living God (Psalms 84:2)." David's heart had a mystical essence to it—to be one with God and to be known by God. The presence of God was everything to him, and in that presence he had access to everything in God's Kingdom.

Through his hunger for more of God and His presence, David moved the heart of God and pulled from heaven to earth what was allotted for another time. David offered sacrifices of praise, worship and prayer to the LORD at the tent of the Ark of the Covenant to the City of David, even though the tabernacle for real sacrifices was somewhere else. He danced mightily and indignantly before the Lord. His prayers were directed like incense and the lifting up of hands like the evening sacrifice.

King David, a type of Christ, was able to recognize the great conflict humanity faces between the soul and the spirit. He learned to strengthen himself in the Lord and teach his soul to submit and listen to the Holy Spirit. Although David did not receive any affection from his earthly father and was despised by his own brothers, God fathered him. He spoke to David directly as a shepherd boy, teaching him how to hear, recognize and trust His voice.

David allowed his history with God to lead him instead of being controlled by public opinion. Even when rising against Goliath, before he struck him dead, David exclaimed, "You come against me with sword and spear and javelin, but I come against you in the name of the Lord Almighty, the God of the armies of Israel, whom you have defied. 46 This day the Lord will deliver you into my hands, and I'll strike you down and cut off your head (1 Samuel 17:45-46)."

Some believe that "the key of David" is the key that unlocks the mysteries of God through a prophetic worship lifestyle. God Himself spoke through the prophet Amos, as declared later by the apostle James in Acts 15, "I will return and rebuild David's fallen tent. Its ruins I will rebuild and I will restore it, that the rest of mankind may seek the Lord, even all the Gentiles who bear my name, says the Lord."

David was a worshipper as both a shepherd boy and a king. He demonstrated that whether one lives a life with very little or a life filled with the riches of a king, worshipping God through instrument, dance, song and lifestyle is the key.

DREAMS

HE RESTORES ALL
Nick Wallace // MDCM Anthology Team // United States

As far back as I can remember I've had dreams. Many of these dreams would be reoccurring, where I would have the same dream multiple times a year for years on end. Or they might be lucid dreams, where I would have full-consciousness, and full emotions in them, feeling more like a vision or a trance than a dream. I would wake up from these not knowing reality, whether what I just saw and experienced was just a dream or something that really happened. The emotions would be so strong that even when I knew it was a dream, it would still take hours or more to get out from under the depression of it.

Unfortunately for me all my dreams growing up were demonic. Every night when I went to sleep someone would be trying to kill or torment me. I had demonic encounters where they would appear in my room while I was awake or in my dreams while I slept. It felt like I couldn't get away from it. Even in the lucid reoccurring dreams, where I knew what was going to happen next, I couldn't change it and even if I tried, it would just end up worse. When I would fall in my dreams, I would hit the ground and not wake up. Or if I were killed I wouldn't wake up; I would just follow around the guy that killed me. It was pure torture at times. I literally had to watch as friends and I were killed or mutilated. Worse yet, I had full emotions and memories in some of the dreams so when I awoke I would just end up carrying the trauma with me.

I struggled for many years because of this torment. It didn't make sense to me why Satan could talk to me so clearly, but I couldn't hear a word from God. I felt like I did something wrong to deserve it. It really put a deep seed of hopelessness in my heart from a young age, which of course led to drugs, a suicidal mentality and many other horrible behaviors. I tell you all this just to show you how influential and powerful dreams and night visions are in affecting the recipient of them. Our dream life is a reality, not a metaphorical world that is meaningless. A third of our life is spent dreaming so it must have relevance. God doesn't make things without purpose. Therefore if relevant, then there must be purpose and power behind dreams and night visions.

It was only 5 years ago that I started hearing the Lord in my dreams. If by the law a thief, Satan, owes us sevenfold what he's stolen, then how much more does he owe us through the law of grace! (Proverbs 6:30 -31)

One of the dreams that began this transformation for me was a dream where I was trapped in Satan's house. I had to watch as one of his ministers destroyed friends and ministries that I knew dearly. In the process of running from the demon, I ran through Satan's sanctuary as I did many other times in the dream. But this time there was a picture hanging on the wall that wasn't there before. The next time I ran through his sanctuary I stopped and noticed the picture was different from everything else in the room. It had many colors on it, and it was a picture of a man's feet.

As I looked more closely, the man's feet turned out to belong to Jesus. The more I focused on His feet something crazy happened: I stopped running! For the first time in my whole life I wasn't running from the enemy in my dream. From then on I had many dreams of facing my enemies and even defeating them and casting them into hell.

Now when I sleep I expect God to show up. I ask Him questions before I go to bed, and He actually answers them. He's given me detailed dreams about friends, family, and people I don't even know. I've also had dreams about how to pray for them or sometimes I've woken up praying or prophesying over certain people.

Even better is that most of the dreams He gives me I don't even have to interpret. They are straightforward, where He tells me to do something or He teaches me something. He's told me that friends would get cars given to them and its happened. One time I had a dream about a house we were about to buy. In the dream the owner of the home is actually an organization of sorts that will not budge on the price, and before I woke up a man began asking me to pray for the owners' salvation. I ended up telling our realtor about the dream and come to find out the house was owned by the Mormon Church, and as it was foretold in the dream they didn't budge on the price!!!

I've been healed in my dreams from sickness, given stock information, and so much more. I've had Kris Vallaton, Bill Johnson, Heidi Baker, Chris Overstreet and many more in my dreams teach me things or prophesy over me. Kris taught me how to cast out demons, break lies, and even rebuked me one time for a false belief I had about God. I've had open visions at night. One time, a radio appeared in my room and started telling me about Isaiah chapter 61. It freaked me out so badly that I tried to get out of the vision. When I did—I thought, "No! Why did I ask Him to leave?! Bring me back! Bring me back!" I've heard His audible voice multiple times now instructing me on how to abide in Him or dispel worries. It's literally endless.

I've been able to see the most beautiful places, houses, mountains, and oceans that are unlike anything I've seen on this earth. I've traveled all over the world, yet these places in my dreams are more beautiful than I could ever even describe or imagine. In some of the dreams, I am breathless with the beauty before me. There are so many colors and details, more than the human mind could ever take in! And when I wake up I can't even come close to recreating what I get to see in my dreams.

I didn't deserve all this goodness. Yet, He is still faithful because He cannot deny Himself (2 Timothy 2:13)! That's what blows me away; He literally only needs a mustard seed of faith and He will do the rest. The reason He asks us for so little faith is because He doesn't want us to take credit for something He paid for! If I had to work hard to conjure up a lot of faith, then I would take more credit for the result of my faith.

What used to be the area of my greatest torment has now become the area of my greatest strength. God can redeem anything. Take note of the greatest areas of attack in your life because that is actually the area of your greatest influence and call. If Satan can discourage us enough in an area of our life and cause enough pain, then we will begin to avoid that area at all costs. But he is trying to get us to lay down our greatest weapon against him and calling on our life. He knows our strength so if he can get us to lay it down, then we won't use it against him.

When God redeems something He will not do it halfway. It will be greater than what the enemy stole. In Joel 2, He says that all of what the swarming locusts have taken will be restored! Take note. Write down your areas of greatest failure. Your greatest struggles will be your greatest victories. That way when victory comes He'll get the credit! For 25 years I was tormented in my sleep. But the last five years have well made up for the 25 taken from me. What's crazy is that this is only the beginning. So, rest and take heart because your victory is dependent upon His goodness, not yours!

ENCOUNTERS IN THE NIGHT
Shannon-Leigh Barry // Mystic // South Africa

I always chuckle at stories of people waiting up at night for God to come. My life never seemed to display a difference between God speaking to me when I was awake or when I was asleep. In fact, my clearest moments of direction have come while I've been sleeping. This is when I know my mind has been switched off from decision-making, and God can show me what He pleases. It started from a young age and a few of the dreams I can remember feel like they happened just yesterday.

The first time I had this particular dream, I remember being around 12 years old. I was in the Anglican Church I grew up attending in South Africa. I was sitting in the second row of pews with my best friend Bronwyn on my left side, another friend William on my right side, and behind me were my parents. People were rushing into the church screaming. I knew it was Judgment Day as there was panic in the atmosphere as people were rushing in. The priest was screaming, "The Lord is coming! The Lord is coming; come inside and shut the windows." He continued, "The Lord's light would burn as it was so bright He did not know who was saved." I began to look around, and I couldn't find my brother. I began weeping on my knees for my brother, as I thought he was lost.

Just then a window above me to my left opened and a bright light came in. As I knelt down weeping, the light touched my hands but I did not burn. My hands actually turned purple. When I awoke the next morning both my hands were purple. They were physically bruised but with no pain. The bruising seemed like a physical manifestation left over from the dream.

I told my mother about the dream and showed her my hands. We had no understanding of what was happening, so we decided to keep quiet about it. In my heart, I longed to know the meaning of what God was saying to me. Later I remembered my purple hands when I was taken to a charismatic church. I asked the Pastor what it could mean. His response was "royalty," and I was saddened by the interpretation. This was not the answer for my dream.

It was more than ten years later before the Lord finally showed me the meaning of the dream. It was about my role in the end times. He explained to me how I would cry to see my brothers and sisters saved, and how He would mark my hands to serve Him. It was through this dream that I would search for salvation and explore the prophetic. This dream marked my life. Now I find myself crying out for the souls of lost brothers. My household, and even my brother, is saved today because I found salvation.

It's amazing how your spirit can have an encounter, and in the moment you have no understanding, but God knows the time and season to reveal to you the very secrets you have kept in your heart.

OPEN PORTALS
Jonathan Louise // Mystic // United Kingdom

A mystical experience that God has highlighted to me happened last Christmas evening when I was in Formby, UK meeting my future in-laws. Firstly, I had a pretty awesome dream where I was in my home church on the second floor. The seats were filled with colorfully dressed modern aristocrats and various leaders. I remember Jason Vallotton was there, smiling at me and saying hello. It was quite a long dream, but all I remember clearly is walking around smiling and enjoying God.

> *"A couple of seconds after sitting up on the mattress, a portal opened in front of me. Instinctively, I put my arms out in front of me and I floated into the portal."*

The cool part happened when my spirit came back to my makeshift bedroom in Formby, but my body was still asleep. It seemed like I was awake, resting in my body, head on my pillow, and looking to my feet. After a few seconds, I had a subtle urge to straighten my feet. When I did, my spiritual feet pointed upward, but my body remained asleep. Then I straightened my knees and felt my spirit legs move, and after that my spirit completely sat up on my mattress while my body still lay there.

The spirit alone has no mind or heart so it feels like pure consciousness. A couple of seconds after sitting up on the mattress, a portal opened in front of me. Instinctively, I put my arms out in front of me and I floated into the portal. On the other side, I was in a silver and purple sparkly mist. Below were cream-colored trees with buds at the end of the branches. I was there for maybe 5 seconds flying or floating when I woke up in the same position when I had left my body.

This was my first full "out of body" experience, and after talking to a couple of fellow mystics, I believe that the spirit realm I went into was the realm of revelation and wisdom, and the trees were in fact neurons (or some mixture of the two). It seems like my spirit can see into and travel to the realm of understanding when I have the grace for it. From this I have been able to know people's thoughts and understand what is in their hearts within my spirit.

That night I went there for real. To be honest, I'm still trying to understand the meaning of this experience. I think I'll need to go to a few more places in the spirit realm to better understand what took place. Something interesting to note is that my intern had a similar experience (but without the portal) when he was my age, as did his mentor before him.

IN WHOSE SEED YOU REMAIN
IS WHOSE SEED YOU BECOME
Nick Wallace // MDCM Anthology Team // United States

A couple years ago, I went through a season where I heard the audible voice of God several times. This was not the "inner audible voice", but this was actually as if someone was in the room talking to me. For the most part, He was just telling me what to believe or to not worry about. Sadly to say, I was actually more afraid of being deceived than actually believing God would talk to me. I was going through a really rough time in my life and wasn't exactly walking with the highest amount of belief. I really didn't think I deserved such an honor, so for months I actually ignored what I heard and thought it had to be demonic.

During one of the encounters that has impacted me the greatest, I heard, "In whose seed you remain, is whose seed you become." After I heard those words, I fell asleep and dreamed that the words were actually creating a people and a world. The world was primitive but growing in response to the words released over it. When I woke up I wrote everything down but really struggled to trust what I heard. Over the next two years, God began unpacking the dream through Scripture, prophetic dreams and other encounters.

The main verse He led me to through another dream was Genesis 22:18 which was a promise to Abraham saying, "By your seed all the nations will be blessed, because you obeyed My Voice." Then He showed me Galatians 3:8, which quotes Genesis 22, "The Scripture, foreseeing that God would justify the Gentiles by faith, preached the gospel beforehand to Abraham, saying "all the Nations will be blessed in you."

Other scriptures that connect to the encounter:

Genesis 3:15	Seed: talking about Christ to come
Mark 4 / Luke 8:4-15	Parable of the Sower; Seed = Word of God
John 1:1 & 14	"The Word was God" and "The Word became flesh and dwelt among us… the only Begotten from the Father full of grace and truth." The Word = Jesus
John 14 & 15	Abiding in Him
Galatians 3	Illustrates the Abrahamic promise we have through Christ. The seed is Christ (verse 16).
1 Peter 1:4	Remaining in His promise = Partaking in His Divine Nature
1 John 3:9	Abiding in His seed = sinless life

And so many more…

God took me through this thread of scriptures to show me what the word "seed" and the audible voice actually meant. He showed me that the same promise Abraham had, we have through Christ! The same gospel that was given to Abraham was the same one Christ preached—the Isaiah 61 gospel of redemption to all oppressed, all afflicted and favor among nations.

Paul further explains it in Galatians 3:14, "He redeemed us in order that the blessing given to Abraham might come to the Gentiles through Christ Jesus, so that by faith we might receive the promise of the Spirit (emphasis added)." Basically, we get what Abraham got, not because we deserve it but through faith alone.

Up until that point, for me all of Christianity was framed under a distorted understanding of "pick up my cross and follow Him." Everything was based upon my performance, what I could do, and what I had to overcome. I understood that I was saved by grace, but the rest of my walk with God turned into me trying to do what He already did.

I literally had given up everything and followed Him! Basically, to me grace became the law on steroids where I prayed for hours to get God's attention or fasted for days to get breakthrough in a particular area. It really led me to a place where Christ and His mission didn't make sense to me. I displayed Christ through my actions but wasn't experiencing any power outside of my own ability. So when I had success, people gave me the credit instead of God.

What I didn't fully grasp is that He did the work, and now my job was to enter into His rest (Ephesians 4). He became the curse to remove it from us. Indirectly, I was saying by my actions that what He did was not enough. I was doing exactly what Paul was reprimanding the Galatians for doing. I accepted His grace for saving me, but from that point forward I took over. I thought that I could prove to God my gratitude by staying away from sin and doing God's work by the strength of my own flesh. There was nothing supernatural about it. It is exactly what the world tries to do. So I had to make up formulas and do A and B in order to get the desired results. Instead of resting in the fact that He was and is the answer, I thought I had to travail for it myself. This whole experience led me to a place of learning to abide in Him, as it says in John 15. As we rest in what He did, we come to a place where things become easy.

All of a sudden, if preparing for a sermon, He downloads one into my heart instead of me having to spend hours just to figure out what to say. Or He's given me the details of how a particular project will go while praying or through a dream, and its actually happened that way. Things begin to happen in such a way that you can't even begin to take credit for it, even our righteousness. The more I choose to rest in Him, the more I start acting like Him. That's what abiding looks like—we rest in Him, and He brings about the fruit.

Practically, it looks like walking in confidence and power knowing that if I step out, He will show up in a way that only He could get the credit for. When we begin to rest in what He did, the supernatural comes easy. It's easier to believe Him for healing or the prophetic because I know it will happen, not based upon my goodness, but because He is good.

"I am the vine; you are the branches. If you remain in me and I in you, you will bear much fruit; apart from me you can do nothing."

John 15:5

ENCOUNTERS IN THE NIGHT // PART TWO
Shannon-Leigh Barry // Mystic // South Africa

I was sleeping in my bedroom back home in South Africa, and I started to burn. My arms were so hot like fire. I couldn't take the heat anymore. I went to the bathroom, still not fully awake yet, and I took a damp towel and put it around me. When I returned to my bed a dewy cloud formed above my bed. I went back to sleep, throwing the covers over me as I tightly wrapped myself in a damp towel, while my body felt like it burned with fire.

This encounter also happened before I was saved. I never knew what the Fire of God was specifically, but at times it would come on me in the night. I would try to rub it off my arms as it burned on my skin, but I had no understanding about Holy Spirit or God encountering me at night. These encounters would continue some years later. I believe many people experience the presence of God but don't understand their encounters. God was visiting me, and I didn't know what this fire was that I felt on my skin. He kept visiting me. At the time, I was praying Jeremiah 29:10 (ESV), "God tells Israel how He will visit them."

Two years ago, I felt the same fire coming on me again. This time I knew God and about manifestations of the Holy Spirit. I was so tired in my bed, but the fire felt like liquid running down my body. I cried at times for it to switch off because it was 3 a.m. and I felt so exhausted. The adrenalin was more than I could bear at times. My heart raced, and I felt like I could run a mile. It's like your physical body cannot contain what's being poured out in that moment, especially a love that is uncompared to any other love. I couldn't ask God to lift it, so I just lay there and tolerated the heat in my body. Eventually I would fall sleep, and when I woke up I would wonder when the fire would sporadically start again.

That experience of feeling fire has now become a reality with dreams and visions in the night happening daily. I expect God to visit in the night. During my first year of ministry school, I would open my bedcovers while the room was dark to find blue electric rays on my sheets. I could see them with my natural eye. The first time it happened, it shocked me so badly that I couldn't sleep.

It was about 4 a.m. and I had just finished a call to South Africa. I trembled getting into the bed as the currents went over my body. It didn't hurt, but it was uncomfortable. The initial electric currents would cause my adrenalin to pump, and then I couldn't sleep. I knew the Presence was waiting for me, so some nights I felt a longing to go to bed because I knew that I would be found there by God's presence. This went on for months, and I realized God knew my sleeping pattern. I asked a friend to sleep in my bed. I watched her as she slept. She was shouting the word fire in her sleep and shaking in the bed. I realized then that I was not crazy!

Recently in a dream, I walked up some stairs in an auditorium, and as I tried to get to my seat, a black man stood up and introduced himself. He said, "Hi, my name is Martin Luther King Jr." and then he introduced his wife to me. He asked me what my name was, and I told him my full name. Then he wrote my name down. It was as if he wanted to get the spelling right. He looked at me and said, "I will remember your name Shannon." I remember thinking in the dream, "Is this real or am I dreaming?" because I could feel the awe of meeting him. He said, "Sit with my wife and I," and then the dream ended.

When I woke up I couldn't get the dream out of my mind because it felt so real to me. I needed to understand what God was saying to me. I asked a friend, but he couldn't interpret it for me, so I asked my friend Nicole if she had any insight. She laughed and told me to open my birthday present. There it was—a book about speeches that change the world, and on the cover was a photo of Martin Luther King Jr. giving his "I have a dream" speech. All I could do was cry. I was overwhelmed that God would tell Nicole to buy that book on my birthday and give me a dream about it before she placed it into my hands. God is so intentional with our dreams and us!

These are some of the most impacting encounters I have had with God. I have come to understand that the Spirit never rests, and God is always speaking. I often hear Him when I'm resting and sleeping. I value what God says at night. I try to write down as much as I can. Sometimes it will be pages full of information, other times it may be just a sentence on what He wants to do or something He is speaking to my heart about.

It can be tiring when you have five or six dreams a night, but to me the night is God's time to talk and it's my time to listen. When I'm sleeping we are having a conversation. So I ask him questions before I fall asleep and expect to wake up with an answer from Him in my spirit. People think being a mystic is about going to heaven, but for me it's been about Him coming to me and desiring to visit me whether it's day or night. I want the way I approach God and the encounters I have with Him to be a daily part of our relationship. Being spiritually minded has to be of earthly good because when God speaks to you, it changes you.

Giordano Bruno
(ca. 1548? – 1600)

"Since I have spread my wings to purpose high,
The more beneath my feet the clouds I see,
The more I give the winds my pinions free,
Spurning the earth and soaring to the sky."

Giordano was a "Dominican friar, philosopher, mathematician, poet, and astrologer[1]." He was known for his ability to memorize lengthy sets of numbers and biblical text by using a memorization technique called loci or memory palace. He was even asked to stand before King Henry III for this ability. Many of his books, like De Umbris Idearum, are still in print today.

Giordano was always a dreamer and a thinker. Many of his ideas challenged the current system of thoughts on theology, the cosmos and other sciences. One of the notions he challenged was that the earth was the center of the universe and that all the planets revolved around us. In a dream, he saw our universe but not the way many of his contemporaries saw it.

He saw that the planets actually revolved around the sun, and that we were not the center but actually in the outskirts of a much vaster solar system. He then lifted up a curtain and saw that beyond ours was an infinite number more solar systems. With this discovery Giordano realized that creation was just as infinite as the Creator2. Many of these theories were not verified until after his death, some by Galileo and others with the invention of the radio telescope in the 1900's.

I do have to mention that although Giordano began well, it is not believed that he ended well. I do not deem that perfect theology gets you to heaven but many of the allegations against him included heresies of extreme nature. God is the only one who ultimately knows, but we can still learn much from his life and legacy as a great example of one who dreamed with God.

1   wikipedia.org/wiki/Giordano_Bruno

2   Cosmos, A Spacetime Odyssey, Episode 1, Standing Up in the
        Milky Way. Directed by Brannon Braga

Dreams in the Bible

Joel 2:28 *"It will come about after this That I will pour out My Spirit on all mankind; And your sons and daughters will prophesy, Your old men will dream dreams, Your young men will see visions."*

Also known as "visions of the night" (Job 33:15), dreams have demonstrated God's desire to interact with and share secrets with His servants even as they sleep. From Abraham to Joseph the father of Jesus, God has spoken with His children through dreams to encourage them, warn them or tell them of things to come. God has even spoken with kings and citizens of other nations to give them messages on behalf of God's servants. In the case of Abimelech, God used a dream to show him the truth about Sarah and then warned him that if he kept Sarah, he would be killed.

Daniel and Joseph gained favor with the kings and leadership of foreign nations through their ability to hear God's voice and interpret dreams. In a dream, Jacob was given instruction on how to favorably mate goats since he had been cheated out of wages many times by Laban. One of the last occurrences of dreams being used in the Bible was with Joseph, the father of Jesus. In Matthew 1:20, it says an angel visited him in a dream to explain to him Mary's pregnancy and the importance of the son that she was carrying.

So whether it is through angels bringing you messages in dreams or God giving you secrets to advance you with favor, God has used dreams in many unusual ways to advance His kingdom and those building it. Sweet dreams!

HEAVEN

LOVE PRESERVES ALL
Ruth Tribhuvan // Mystic // India

In October 2013, God took me to the third heaven in an encounter that lasted for 6 hours (although it only actually felt like 20 minutes to me). In this encounter, He showed me His relationship with the prophets, disciples and elders. There is so much friendship between them. They laugh and joke with each other. They would die for each other. Jesus knew how to die for them, and they knew how to die for Jesus. Friends die for each other. Jesus said "there is no greater love than to lay down one's life for a friend" (John 15:13). We are called to be friends and lovers of Jesus.

"I also saw Jeremiah, and he was so full of joy. It is a standing joke in heaven that people on earth call Jeremiah "the weeping prophet" because he is actually so happy!"

The heart of heaven is an encounter of love. Love is a person. Love is Jesus. He is a blazing fire of love. When you get a glimpse of this truth, everything else becomes an inferior reality. Nothing in this world has the love of Jesus. Jesus looks at the prophets as friends, and He calls them into council for making decisions. I saw a round table and decision-making was going on. God was not making all the decisions, but He was asking His friends what they thought. In my encounter, I also saw Jeremiah, and he was so full of joy. It is a standing joke in heaven that people on earth call Jeremiah "the weeping prophet" because he is actually so happy!

The Lord wants us to know what it means to be royalty, and He wants each one of us to have access to the throne room. We have this access through

Jesus and our relationship with Him. Everyone is a mystic in some sense—as everyone is called to live in more than one reality. Heaven's reality is more real than what we can see in this world. There can be a breakdown in this physical reality, but there is never a breakdown in the heaven's reality. There is never a breakdown!

Jesus has made love an indestructible reality. Loves preserves everything. Love always wins, and it is indestructible. We have authority to call things we see around us into alignment with heaven. The angelic realm is available to carry out decisions made in heaven.

We are the gates of heaven. Wherever you are, you are a gate of heaven. And wherever you stand, you release the decisions of heaven. We need to call things into alignment with the Kingdom of God. You don't need to be a "mystic" to do this; you just need to be a lover of Jesus. Jesus wants the Church to stop playing on the defense and to start playing on the offense. Heaven is invading, therefore, we are to be on the offensive. If you see something in Heaven, then God is calling you to bring that to earth.

Once I saw the devil standing with a bucket load of prayers, and they all belonged to him, because these prayers had come out of a spirit of fear and striving. These prayers were going unanswered. We need to pray from a position of power. Thankfulness is important because it gives ownership of our prayers to God. The devil is only as strong as our agreement with him.

When you are in the third heaven, the second heaven is under your feet! We do not need to strive with fighting the demonic because it is already under our feet. Sometimes we see intercession as striving and pleading, but this is not the case. We are supposed to stand in the throne room without striving, because we have been given power to bring heaven's reality to earth.

EMBASSY OF HEAVEN
Brian Corbin // Mystic // United States

A few years back, I was working an XP Media conference with Jacob (not a real name for privacy purposes), Joshua Mills, John Crowder, and Jamie Galloway. One of the nights, Patricia invited us to the green room to hang out and eat with Joshua Mills and Jacob. So we sat down, and Jacob began to unload some of the crazy encounters and deep revelations he has received over the years. After being there for a while, we realized it was getting late. But as we got up to leave, Jacob asked us if we wanted to hang out in his hotel room. As you can imagine, excitedly, we said yes!

As we were heading to his room, we got into the elevator and he started asking us if we know what an embassy is. He then started telling us that his room is like the embassy of Heaven, and that when we get there it might feel a bit weird and we will have to adjust. If I knew then what I know now, I probably would not have been laughing to myself as he told us that. When we got to his hotel room door, he asked us to stand there for a minute. As we waited we began feeling heat come from the door in waves. It was like being next to a sub-woofer, feeling the vibrations but not hearing the noise, just the heat and vibration. As you can imagine, we were getting pretty excited at this point.

When we walked into the room, it looked like a normal hotel room. There was nothing special about the room, but when we were in there he told us to acclimate to the environment. As soon as he said that we all started to tilt sideways—literally not able to stand up straight. It was almost like being tipped upside down. It was the weirdest experience. We were walking around the room slanted and just looking at each other in awe. Jacob was over in the corner just laughing and thinking the whole thing was funny. As we were talking to each other we kept saying, "It is so odd being flipped upside down." But Jacob corrected us and said, "Actually you are finally right side up. You've been upside down your whole life but in this environment, the Embassy of Heaven, you are being flipped right side up." It felt like being disoriented where your equilibrium won't normalize.

When we finally adjusted, Jacob began downloading even more revelation of the Father and how things really work here on earth. He was speaking so fast it was like he was talking at a million miles an hour. I was floored the whole time he was talking because we were able to keep up and understand what he was saying. He then explained to us that in this environment there are no hindrances so what might be difficult to comprehend under normal circumstances would be easier in the presence of God. It felt like being in the Matrix—being plugged into the machine where things were just downloaded into your head. And he said, "Don't worry about remembering all that I've shared with you because it is being downloaded into your spirit man. The Holy Spirit will bring it back to you whether you think you have it or not."

Then he asked us if we wanted to see something really cool—as if what we had already seen wasn't amazing enough. Jacob sat on the edge of his bed and asked me to sit in his desk chair. I was sitting directly across from him, and he asked me to stare directly into his eyes. He then told me if I felt the urge to look away or something else happened, to just try to focus on his eyes. I was staring into his eyes, and all of a sudden I saw his face begin to shift, which caused me to blink and lose my focus. He told me that I almost had it and to try again, but he said, not to look away this time.

He knew the level of what I was seeing. It was kind of crazy that he knew exactly where I was at spiritually. He could tell how far I was getting, and how far I was away from understanding what he was going to show me. We tried again, and his face began to shift again. I started freaking out a bit, and finally his face completely turned into a totally different face. My friend shouted to me that he was seeing the change too. Jacob's face transformed into a brilliantly bright white, most beautiful face I have ever seen. It just completely drew us in. We asked him what we were looking at, and he told us that he was manifesting his spirit man on the outside so we could see what he looked like. He then told us that this is how we are supposed to see each other all the time. We are supposed to see each other as we are in the spirit through the Spirit of God. Wow!

Next he asked us if we wanted to have a third heaven encounter with him. So we all lay down on the floor, and he started mentoring us on how to experience heaven. I had done this before but not to this extreme! When we arrived in heaven, we were able to walk around and see each other in the spirit. The way we looked in Heaven did not look anything like the way we looked in the natural, but I was able to discern who each person was. The whole time we were walking around, Jacob was acting like he'd been there many times before.

We went to the library of heaven, and he asked us to start reading aloud the titles of the books. All the titles were pretty bizarre, but he kept asking us, "What is the Holy Spirit telling you to do with the books?" One guy said, "I feel like we are supposed to shove them into my stomach!" Jacob said, "Yeah, eat the scroll" (Ezekiel 3:1)! We walked around reading titles of books and shoving them into our stomachs the whole time.

Then Jacob took us into a river where we could breathe under the water in addition to going to many other places. Finally we left, and he asked us if we wanted to fly somewhere. I was trying and trying to fly and basically got nowhere. I asked, "Why can't I get off the ground?" He said, "You are trying to do it in your own strength. You are just supposed to yield to the Father." As soon as I did this, I just took off in flight.

When we got off the floor, it felt like 12 hours or more had gone by. You would have thought we were there all night and into the next day—that is how long it felt like we were encountering heaven. When we looked outside, the sun was not even up yet. It was only four in the morning, and we didn't even leave to go to the hotel room until after midnight earlier than night. The 12 hours we thought we were gone for was actually just 4 or so! How did only a few hours go by?! Jacob said, "That is what I've been trying to tell you, in heaven you are literally outside of time! So we were able to do a ton of things that you would not have been able to do if we were in earth's natural time." He then told us to hurry and follow him into the bathroom. When we got into the bathroom, we looked in the mirror and our faces were glowing! All of us were glowing! (Exodus 34:35 – Moses' face shown after meeting with the Lord on Mt. Sinai)

As we were leaving to go to our hotel, he told us to be aware that since we'd had a lot of things imparted to us, we might notice being able to read people's thoughts now and a bunch of other strange or radical occurrences might start happening. Jacob said, "But here is the thing, the way God can trust you with what you've been given tonight is by how much integrity you have with what you've been given. So if you are hearing people's thoughts, then make sure you don't use it against them or to manipulate them. How you steward this will show God whether you can be entrusted with more. That shows God the level at which He can trust you."

We appreciated how real Jacob was being with us. He was not trying to be mean but just really honest. He told us if we want to be trusted with more, then we have to be faithful with what He's given us. Our trustworthiness will show by our integrity, how we steward our gifts and by how we honor God and others with them. It was so powerful, and even after we left I was still buzzing.

That day going forward was a pivotal point in my life because God started opening up some deep revelation to me. When I share my revelations with others I mostly get weird looks, but it's stuff that science hasn't been able to prove yet. I don't really argue with people. But I feel like I see so much more clearly now, so I have to adjust to the shift that happened in my life. Some people totally understand this, but some just don't think what I experienced seems possible.

I am learning a lot, but I'm also always being stretched in new ways. Because of this my intimacy and trust in God has gone to a whole new level. He would continually confirm revelation that He was showing me through the prophets or many different avenues. God completely opened a whole new realm to me through this journey.

The confirmations helped me see that I was not crazy, especially because I was hearing revelation that not everyone else was hearing. God is bringing to light what has not been revealed to the masses yet. It is like being a forerunner and hearing those deep things ahead of time. Jacob has so much child-like faith, and he makes room to have fun. He knows really well how to be a son and have intimacy with the Father through humility.

We are living in a time where God wants to reveal to us deep revelation. These revelations are for the church but most of the church is still trying to decide if healing is even for today, so it is hard to go deeper when stuck on such shallow theology. God is saying there is so much more He wants to reveal to us that goes far beyond healing. It made me sad when I heard Jacob's heart about this because there is so much God wants to give us, as His kids, to understand and encounter Him. But fear can hold us back and limit us to the basics. For some people, mystical revelation is too "out of the box" and really just seems too good to be true. This whole experience took me out of my own box and helped me see what religion really looks like.

Throughout history there have been beliefs in some parts of the collective church that are actually religious or demonic doctrine being accepted as truth. We've allowed this because we are so indoctrinated with lies, fears and shame that we've actually interpreted things in Scripture as truth, which are actually perversions of what God wanted for us. We've allowed shame to disqualify us or create rules that God never intended.

For example, one of the areas that God has really been teaching me about is sexuality. This is the one area that I've noticed the Lord bringing me revelation about the most. I have mentored guys regarding their sexuality for years while working for a college ministry. The Lord had to correct some of my own beliefs about sexuality because what I was teaching to be purity was actually false religious doctrine. The Lord began showing me that my perspective was drenched in shame. He showed me how mistakes in my life and in my leaders' lives as well as other teachings had skewed my perspective on this topic. My skewed perspective led me to defining purity out of fear and religious tradition, not truth.

These wrong definitions have existed in the church for centuries, and I can actually pin point how we started this journey in the wrong direction. The enemy tried to bring confusion to shame sex in the church to the point that the church stopped talking about it. This fear-based perspective on sexuality has led the church into a distorted view of it.

Armed with new knowledge, I've seen a lot of individuals set free in this area. When they finally see their sexuality the way it's supposed to look and when they understand why He made their body the way He did, all the lies we've believed over the years finally get exposed leading to inner healing. Inner healing allows people to receive a full perspective on themselves and God's perspective on their sexuality. It also allows them to have radical intimacy with God, and only in intimacy can we have freedom! That is why I'm really fighting for true revelation on this topic because I want to see healthy families and individuals. This is one of the last areas the church really needs breakthrough in for us to see radical revival.

God is trying to show us that the freedom and authority He has for us is truly limitless, because He trusts us and it's based on His love, not ours. The encounter I had in heaven directly influenced this revelation I received on earth. When I saw heaven I was finally able to see earth for what it truly is, and was finally able to see the people of earth the way our Father does, with love.

Listen to Audio

John the Apostle
(ca. 6 - 100)

John, the son of Zebedee, was one of the first men Jesus called to follow him. Along with his father and brother James, John was a fisherman at the Sea of Galilee. Like Peter, John was among the closest of Jesus' disciples and later became a leading apostle and father of the faith.

The book of Revelation or Apocalypse is a vivid symbolic vision of the end times that John had while in prison at Patmos. The visions are filled with symbolism inspired by Old Testament prophetic writings from Daniel, Ezekiel and Zachariah. In these visions, John had several visions of heaven—two can be found in the fourth and twenty-first chapters of Revelations. Below is just a piece of one of his visions of heaven.

Revelations 4:1-4 "After these things I looked, and behold, a door standing open in heaven, and the first voice which I had heard, like the sound of a trumpet speaking with me, said, "Come up here, and I will show you what must take place after these things." 2 Immediately I was in the Spirit; and behold, a throne was standing in heaven, and One sitting on the throne. 3 And He who was sitting was like a jasper stone and a sardius in appearance; and there was a rainbow around the throne, like an emerald in appearance. 4 Around the throne were twenty-four thrones; and upon the thrones I saw twenty-four elders sitting, clothed in white garments, and golden crowns on their heads."

Elisha and his servant, Ezekiel, Jesus, Paul and Stephen were also given glimpses into heaven before their time to enter. Heaven gives us the model for how we are to influence earth. As the scripture Matthew 6:10 states, "Your kingdom come, your will be done, on earth as it is in heaven." God reveals here that His will is for earth to become like heaven. So, let us take a glimpse at heaven and never look at earth the same.

MIRACLES

KEYS TO EVERY DOOR
Geen George Varghese // Mystic // India

I had a season in my life where a lot of people came to me and gave me keys—sometimes they were just pictures of keys and sometimes they were real keys. I had no idea what this meant! Then one day I had an encounter in my prayer time where Jesus had keys for every door. Jesus was able to open and close every door. I asked Jesus how I could have access to these keys; He said that I have access when I partner with the Holy Spirit!

Jesus has the key for heaven, hell, life and death. The enemy lost the key! One time, Jesus showed me His key for unlocking finances. After that I saw a lot of breakthrough in the area of finances. This revelation opened the door for financial miracles in my life. I have attended three years of BSSM and all of it has been a financial miracle. God has not just given me enough to live on, but I have had more than enough. I have only worked for a month during three years of school.

Some people have paid for my mission trips and tuition because they felt like God wanted them to. God has even sent people to buy me the exact groceries I needed, and they even brought them to my door. I have told nobody my needs. One day somebody came to me and said, "I want to buy you a car!"

I feel like this happens because there is always enough in the Kingdom. The door for the storehouses of heaven is open for all His children. Now when I pray for other people, they see financial miracles as well.

When it comes to hell, I see miracles because Jesus turned everything over on the cross. I have seen great miracles where people were raised from the dead. In the last three weeks, I have seen three people come back from dead or being in a coma. One person's body was considered clinically dead, and I watched them come back to life! I see lots of creative miracles because Jesus has this key. He gave us the keys for everything. It doesn't matter how big a door is—even a small key can unlock a big door.

One time I was hanging out with some friends, and we were having a wonderful evening together. Later we went outside and were just watching the stars. We prayed that the stars would become bigger, and they actually appeared bigger. We can do things like this because He loves us so much!

"In the last three weeks, I have seen three people come back from the dead or being in a coma."

The Father gave us the Holy Spirit because He is the only one who has access to the heart of God. I expect to have conversations with the Holy Spirit all the time. Sometimes He inspires me with cooking recipes or poems or basically anything you can think of! The most mystical people don't always talk about their experiences unless you ask them.

A mystic knows that in God we have no limitations. This includes money and time!

DISNEYLAND REVIVAL
Jason Chin // Mystic // United States

During my first year of School of Supernatural Ministry, they were teaching us how to dream with God. In these exercises, we were supposed to dream without any limits. One of the activations they had for us was posing the question, "If money was not an issue, there were no limits, you could not fail and you had no fear—what would you love to see happen in your life?" But what happened is that I would actually start taking this on as homework. So in my bedroom while I was in first year of BSSM, I would lay on my bed and dream with God.

I would imagine wild break-outs of revival or imagine myself in an airplane where someone would get healed, and then the whole plane would get saved and gold dust would show up. In these wild dreams, I would also think about going down to Disneyland and practicing words of knowledge on all the people waiting in line for rides, praying for the sick and seeing God do great miracles. I would just dream these daydreams like a little child in my room.

About a year later, I was driving down to Los Angeles and saw a billboard sign with Mickey Mouse on it fighting a dragon with a flaming sword. I thought to myself, "Father, it would be so cool if that really happened someday at Disneyland." I arrived to L.A. and I met with a friend and spoke at his church. At the end of the night, a lady walked up to me and my friends after the service and asked us if we wanted to go to Disneyland the next day because she had a bunch of free tickets. The next day when we got to Disneyland, we started to pray for people right away. At first it was really slow—people didn't want prayer or when they did get prayer they might get partially healed, or one lady got completely healed, but when we told her it was Jesus she freaked out and the whole group ran away.

Finally, we went to the food court, and we noticed a guy wearing a blue arm sling. We walked up to him to ask him what happened to his arm. It turns out he was the star quarterback for his junior high school football team, and he had a torn rotator cuff. So my friend and I just prayed for him, and instantly he got completely healed. We asked him to take his sling off, and he lifted his arm over his head with a look of shock and unbelief on his face. He froze, so we asked him what was happening to him. He started crying and said, "I couldn't lift my arm more than an inch this morning." We told him that Jesus loved him, that the same Jesus in the Bible was the one that healed him just then, and we shared the gospel with him.

Surrounding him were about eight of his friends, so we turned and started praying for them. Before we knew what was happening legs were growing out and kids were getting healed. We told them that Jesus didn't come just to heal them but to save them and He wanted all of their lives, not just part. All the kids asked Jesus to come into their hearts! Half of them had never been saved but the other half rededicated their lives to Jesus. After that, we had them encounter the Holy Spirit's Presence by lifting their hands up and asking the Holy Spirit to come in a way that they could physically feel Him.

When we were finished with that group, we went on our way and got some food. Not much later, I got a tap on my shoulder and the same kids, plus 10 more teens, are standing behind us. They start telling us about different injuries they had and how they wanted their friends to feel the Holy Spirit too. So we told the first group of kids, "You have the same equipment that we do to see Jesus heal people, so you should pray for them to get healed. We don't have anything that you don't." When the first group laid their hands on the second group miracles instantly started to happen. One of the girls had knees that would knock together to the point that she never was able to run. We literally saw her legs straighten and watched her run for the first time that she could remember.

Other dramatic miracles started to happen, like bone spurs and bumps would dissolve, and kids would get covered in gold dust. Then the kids started calling their other friends and telling them they needed to get to the food court. This lasted for about four hours, and the group just kept growing and growing. We saw about 120 instantaneous miracles. There were dramatic miracles like deformed rib cages being completely reformed. About 80 to 100 kids gave their lives to the Lord that day.

A few days later, our friend posted a video of some of the healings on You Tube. We began hearing stories of different youth groups playing this video and having healing services in churches, out on the streets and even in emergency rooms. About a year ago, I got a phone call from the football player that we first prayed for at Disneyland. He told me he was now in Bible school and wanted to be a missionary. One thing the Lord taught me through all of this is that dreaming and creation are closely related. Even in Hebrew, the word for imagination, *yetser* and the word for creation, *yatsar*, are nearly spelled the same. There is a powerful link between seeing it in your heart and it becoming a reality in the natural, hence why Paul in 2 Corinthians calls us to "hold every thought captive."

The Lord really loves when we dream with Him. We abide in Him and He abides in us, so when we dream, He creates with us. I want my life to be spent captivating my heart and imagination with what's on His heart and imagination. Through this we come one step closer to being "co-laborers" with Christ. When you give Him your heart and mind, you'll soon discover your actions following! No longer do we just talk about Him, but we demonstrate that He is here now as the Living God.

Disneyland Revival video March 28th 2012

Lovesaysgo.com

St. Anthony of Padua
(ca. 1195 – 1231)

"A Christian's greatest danger is preaching and not practicing, believing but not living according to what he believes."

Born in Portugal, St. Anthony entered a monastery at the age of 15 and spent the next 10 years dedicating his life to quiet study and prayer. Eventually St. Anthony began preaching, and his preaching was filled with wonderful revelations from the Holy Spirit.

One time, St Anthony was attempting to preach, but a large group of hecklers kept disrupting him. Therefore, he decided to preach to the fish instead! He told the fish in the nearby water to "come and hear the word of God." It is then reported that hundreds of fish gathered and listened most attentively to his message with their heads popping up out of the water! Finally, St. Anthony sent the fish on their way with a blessing. This miracle impacted many of the onlookers who then returned to faith.

Another time, St. Anthony was going to preach to more than 30,000 people in a Roman amphitheatre. However, as he started to preach, a violent storm was about to break out. When people began leaving in anticipation of the impending storm, St. Anthony said to them, "Have confidence in God. I assure you in His name that He will not let one of you get wet". No rain fell in the amphitheatre, and the crowd stayed to listen to his message. When the crowd later left the amphitheatre, they discovered that the area outside was flooded and covered with large hailstones!

Miracles in the Bible

Mark 16:20 *"Then the disciples went out and preached everywhere, and the Lord worked with them and confirmed His word by the signs that accompanied it."*

Ultimately God is sovereign, and nothing makes this more apparent than a miracle. It is literally an act that is completely outside of humanity's realm of understanding and ability. Miracles seem to break all the laws of physics and mathematics that we like to neatly package our world in. They seem to utterly shatter all formulas and leave process and tradition scratching their heads when it's all been said and done. Some of the most interesting miracles in the Bible were the ones that made the least amount of sense. God can literally show up however He pleases, yet He chose to make a donkey talk to Balaam and His son Jesus' first miracle was getting drunken people more drunk! Why did God choose to use a burning bush with Moses, dry bones to teach Ezekiel how to prophesy, or have Elijah run faster than a chariot? Couldn't there have been an easier way to communicate what He wanted them to know, or what was the purpose of Elijah running faster than a chariot?

Miracles will always leave us in awe whether we are the recipients of them or the one God humbly uses to release them. But in the end, miracles do not have to be understood because they were never meant to be our focus. Their only purpose is to bring our attention back to their Creator. If we could understand and control everything, why would we ever need Him? Miracles will always remind us of our dependency on the Miracle Maker.

OTHER

SPIRIT REALM REALITY
Sheldon Watrous // Mystic // United States

The spiritual realm is real. Therefore, the supernatural is not something abstract but actually a very concrete realm that we know little about. It was March 28th, 2012 and we were doing some street ministry all day and saw very little happen. But for whatever reason, I had this expectation that the evening would be one of our best ever. So we went to a casino and right off the bat, we saw a guy get saved, another guy with a broken leg get healed, and another lady set free of gambling addictions.

When we sat down to eat, I heard the voice of the Lord say, "There is a lady here who has a daughter that sings and dances." So I asked the waitress if she had a kid that loves to sing and dance. Come to find out, not only did she not have a kid, she was single and didn't even want to have kids. "It's the farthest thing from what I want right now in my life," she said. But she continued, "Why do you ask?" I told her that sometimes the Lord gives me bits of information for people to bless them and let them know He cares.

Come to find out, she was a Muslim, and she could see in the spirit realm how people will get injured or die. At this point, one of our teammates asked if she had pain in her feet. She did and I told her, "If we pray for you right now, you will be healed." After she agreed, I prayed for her and instantly her feet felt better. She said, "I've never felt that. How did you do that?" So we told her that it's all about Jesus and how much He loves her. We blessed her with prayer, helped her clean up and moved on to pray for others.

I thought we would never see her again, but about two hours later the same lady tracked us down saying, "When you prayed for me, I never felt something so powerful. It was almost as if my spirit was spinning forwards." She then began to tell us how her spirit has always spun backwards, and she feels like its going down the wrong spiral. I said, "Its just God you were experiencing." She replied, "No, you don't understand, when I tried to see into your life to see how you were going to get hurt or injured, all I saw was a giant wall of light that would not let me see through or pass it... what is that?" I told her it's the Holy Spirit living in me, and He protects me from anything. But she interrupted saying, "You need to pray for me because my kidneys are inflamed and in a lot of pain."

After we prayed, her kidney pain went away and she asked us how we kept doing this. She then told us about her Muslim faith, Muhammad, and also how every night before bed she sees a man that looks like Allah who threatens to kill her. We told her that Allah is a false god, Muhammad is a false prophet, and the only way to true salvation and heaven is through Jesus Christ. I said to her, "If you would like, right now, you can receive the Lord Jesus and all those things will be taken away. You have been healed twice now so you know all those things can be gone. Would you like to receive Jesus?"

As we were leading her through prayer to receive Jesus, she kept getting to His name and wasn't able to say it. She kept fighting to say "Jesus" but couldn't, so we asked her to try spelling His name. After she spelled it we asked her if she would like the same wall of light that protects us to protect her. Again she said yes, and we led her to invite the Holy Spirit into her life. The whole time we were praying she kept asking us to stop because she felt like the Spirit we were imparting to her was too strong. She kept thinking she was going to fall over. Finally she stopped us and ran to the bathroom! This whole night just kept getting crazier and crazier. When she returned, she told us that she went into the bathroom to vomit and brown-black-green stuff came out of her mouth. Basically, she vomited out every bad spirit she had been inviting in order to have divinations. We then gave her a Bible and connected her to a church nearby.

When we talked to her a week later, she said all her regular customers kept saying there was something different about her, like she's lost weight or her skin was glowing. But her reply was, "It's just God." She is now into intercessory prayer, and since then she has gotten perfect sleep and is no longer attacked by the demon at night.

This encounter makes me completely in love with God, and it shows me how real the spiritual realm is! Even if we don't see it, it's all around us. This lady had physical signs of her encounters with the demonic and then with the Holy Spirit. Both had severely different ramifications on her physical body and overall well-being. Since then, I've had a couple other interactions with people that have seen the same wall of light protecting me, which shows me that literally, "The Spirit who lives in you is greater than the spirit who lives in the world" (1 John 4:4 NLT).

We don't have to have it all together before we start ministering to the lost. Our testimony started because I got a word of knowledge wrong! But I took the risk, and I kept pointing back to the Father and His love. And He took my wrong and made it a right! I've seen a lot of salvations, but never had I seen one so authentic before, and it's part of the reason I'm so passionate now to see people saved.

This experience made my boldness grow because I realized that not only is the Holy Spirit with us, but He is our protector. So when I go to minister, I don't fear because I know Who is protecting me. It's crazy to me how tangible He really is and how accessible He is. To me the term mystic means to be in constant communion with the Lord and when He says "speak," then I speak. I don't have to get it perfectly right because my ministry is directed towards Him.

When I step out, if I rest in the fact that I'm accepted, then I will never fail. It is not as big of a deal to Him whether you hear Him perfectly every time, but He cares more that you take a risk. This awareness of His acceptance of me whether I get something right or not is what gives me boldness because "perfect love casts out fear" (1 John 4:18 NASB). We have to understand that if God says to step out, then we should do it because the reward is so much greater than the risk will ever be.

Listen to Audio

VISION FOR THE NATIONS
Sandy Hawk // Mystic // United States

During an encounter on November 7, 2013 Jesus gave me a crystal globe on which all the nations of the earth were detailed and highlighted. When I asked Jesus what it meant He said, "Pray and bless the spirit of the leaders of every nation. Bless their governmental mantles."

From this, I compiled a prayer book with all 196 national leaders' names, pictures and a map of their nation. I included a one-line blessing for each of them. I feel God is saying to the Church...

"Because the Church has stewarded well the revival over the last 20 years, we are in a position to stand on the next greater wave of His Spirit. The individual Christian will walk in such an anointing and power that individuals will not be exalted over the other, because everyone will be healing, evangelizing, and raising the dead. The only dividing line will be Christian and 'Pre-Christian.' Denominationalism will be broken down."

RECKLESS ABANDONMENT
Kalina Georgieva // MDCM Anthology Team // United Kingdom

The God of the Impossible is unstoppable in revealing His heart which releases and enables us to enter into and possess our unshakeable inheritance of being His beloved royal family-not only in the UK but throughout the world! In this audio I have shared only parts of my life transforming exchange with Him in the Moravian Falls at Thanksgiving 2013. It is not about me, but it is all about His glory through His burning holy fire, unfailing love and faithfulness.

I pray that this story would impart greater hunger in all of us for living in the fullness of His presence through intimate communion with Him. I also pray that it would empower many more hearts to live out recklessly abandoned to His call and purposes here and now for the nations of the world to experience our God of the impossible like never before. What happened during those few days is strongly rooted in scripture. It shows how He longs to co-create with us and has all the power to change history through us by the resurrection power of His Cross and the breath of His Holy Spirit in us.

Listen to Audio

St. Dominic
(ca. 1170 – 1221)

St. Dominic was known for his study of scriptures, devotion to prayer, and he would often be seen weeping for sinners and for the needy. He founded the institute for women at Prouille, and dedicated his life to preaching and converting a sect known as the Albigensians, after they murdered a papal legate.

One time St. Dominic was challenged by the heretic Albigensians. Among other things, this sect denied the humanity of Christ, prohibited all procreation and endorsed suicide. For the challenge, the Albeigensian's proposed that they and St. Dominic write their beliefs into a book, and then present them to a panel of judges. However, after reviewing the opposing beliefs, the judges refused to give a decision. As such, the Albigensians then proposed that the books be thrown into a fire, so that God could decide which beliefs were correct!

"And the two volumes were cast therein; that of the heretics was immediately consumed to ashes; the other, which had been written by the blessed man of God, Dominic, not only remained unhurt, but was borne upward by the flames in the presence of the whole assembly. Again, a second and a third time they threw it into the fire and each time the same result clearly manifested which was the true faith, and the holiness of the man who had written the book1." St. Dominic led a life that demonstrated his devotion toward God. He didn't just talk of God's miraculous intervention but he positioned himself in a way that was in constant need of it.

1   Drane, The Life of St. Dominic, TAN Books 1988, page 16

THE PROCESS

COMING TO JESUS
Joaquin Evans // Mystic // United States

The Encounter

The first major encounter I had with God took place in 2001. I would say this is what really established what my walk and ministry would look like. In one sense it was my introduction into the kingdom. A year and a half earlier, I said the sinner's prayer and really meant it but didn't have an internal transformation really happen at that point. The roots of my faith were there so something started to germinate, but this encounter is what radically changed me.

Basically, I entered a season where the Lord started to speak to me, which was weird because I didn't grow up in church or have that sort of history with the Lord. My life was actually running in the exact opposite direction until a friend invited me to a David Hogan meeting. At this event, I said the sinner's prayer, which was a pretty good start. But now a year or so later, God was telling me that I'd had enough time to flounder, "You said the prayer, now let's get serious." God speaking to me this way was completely odd, especially because He we speaking to me through the inner audible voice of God on a number of occasions. I had never experienced anything like this before so it really confused me and threw me off.

Then one night I had a dream about serving God, which was odd for someone completely un-churched. When I awoke from the dream, the Lord said, "Call Rene." Rene was an old roommate of mine during college. When I called her, the first thing I said is, "How's God?" Which was the last thing she ever expected to hear me say! Since college she had gotten saved and was baptized in the Holy Spirit. She went crazy and started telling me everything she'd been doing the last year since she was born again.

When I hung up with her, I said, "What is going on?!" This voice just started talking to me and saying stuff like, "Call Rene," and when I called her I found out that her whole life had been changed by God—this was just getting crazy!

Then my friend, Eddy, that invited me to the David Hogan meeting, called me right after I was done talking to Rene and told me that he was coming into town that weekend for a work convention. He asked if he could stay with me. Not only that, but Rene was also coming into town the same weekend. So the only two people I knew in the world that were full of this Holy Ghost stuff were coming into town randomly the same weekend.

When we met up, they started telling testimonies about God and about how amazing He is. As they were talking, the Presence of God began hovering over the table. I don't know what it was, but all I know is that I had this cheesy smile as they were talking back and forth. At one point, they looked at me and asked what I was smiling about. I said, "I don't know; I just feel really good."

When we finally left the restaurant, there was a homeless lady sleeping in the doorway of a shop nearby. The inner audible voice said to me, "Give her two dollars and tell her that I love her." As I was saying to myself, "That was a really weird thought. Where did that come from?" Eddy stops, turns around and gives the lady two dollars and begins to tell her how much God loves her. When he said that, she sat up from her sleeping bag. She had a Bible clutched to her chest, and she started weeping. This is the moment when I thought it was all crazy! I had to figure out what's going on. So I told the two of them I had to hang out with them until I figured out everything there was to know about the Holy Spirit.

The next week, Eddy asked me if I wanted to attend a youth conference that some local churches were putting on. After he called the youth pastor,

Eddy told me that I could go, but I would have to come as a youth counselor. I was thinking to myself: I've only been to one church meeting ever, and now you are going to take me as a counselor!?

When we showed up at the youth event I wasn't out of the car for more than a minute when a fight broke out between two kids. Nobody noticed this but me, even though there were counselors all around! Nobody else saw it, and I was thinking, "What is happening? This is not what I thought Christian church camp was going to be like." So I stood in the circle watching and perplexed. From watching, I found out that three of the kids were brothers in a gang and their mom forced them to come to the camp. Basically, they were just going to run away until another kid from the camp found out and tried to stop them. The kid from the gang was telling the other Bible camp kid, "You can't tell me anything about life. You've never drunk a beer, you've never been high, and you've never slept with a girl!"

I was listening to this when all of a sudden words came out of me that I had no intention of saying. I was just standing there dumb-founded and then I heard myself saying, "Hey, you're talking about all this stuff you've done, so let me tell you that I've done ten times more in all those realms." Then I started comparing God to being better than getting high with friends. I used this whole analogy about how a high only lasts so long before you have to get more and so on.

I told them that being with God is like being high all the time! Again, it was crazy because I didn't have a grid for these words that came out of me. After I was done talking, the kid in the gang told me they wouldn't run away now, but if they were going to stay, then they wanted to hang out with me all weekend. At this point, I didn't even know how saved I was or where these words were even coming from, but I said, "Alright!"

The next day during worship I had this conversation with God saying, "If You are really real, then I want to know You. If You are real then show up; do something. Prove it." I prayed that during the whole first and second session but nothing happened.

During the third session I was standing in the back and I prayed the same thing. I heard that same inner audible voice and it said, "You need to be humble." At this point worship was about to end, so I prayed the most dangerous prayer I could pray, "Okay God, humble me." And in response, God told me that I needed to get low. So I put my chin down on my chest, but the voice said, "You need to get lower." So I bent at the waist but the voice again said, "You need to get lower." So I sat down in my chair and the voice was still telling me to get lower. I ended up in an airplane crash position with my head between my knees, but the voice was still saying to get lower in a loving but stern voice. Then it hit me that God wanted me to go face first on the floor.

He was asking for an action of complete surrender, but I was too embarrassed because I'd never been in church before. I didn't want to get on the floor in front of all those people. So I was having a dialogue with God while my head was still between my knees. The guy that was speaking said, "I had this encounter with God a year before on this same day. The Lord walked into my bedroom and said, 'This generation is going to be the captain of the army of final harvest.'"

Now I hadn't heard a word he'd said before that comment, but when he said that it was like an invisible layer in the heavens split open. Something cracked open and a physically warm liquid love began to pour in and over my body, from the top of my head, over my shoulders and all through me. It was like the raw physical expression of love oozed through my body, and I started to cry in response to what was happening to me.

The Lord again told me that I still wasn't low enough. I said, "Lord, I don't know what to do. I don't want to be on the floor in front of these kids. God, I don't know what to do." Then the speaker stopped what he was saying earlier and said, "You know I feel like the Lord is saying people need to come and humble themselves on the floor before God."

I had this liquid love oozing through my body, tears were coming down my face, and when he said that it took me a minute to realize that he was talking to me. But the speaker had already started to talk again and nobody responded. So now I said, "God, I know that was for me, but if that was really from You, then have him say it again." Then the guy stopped speaking again and said, "No—God is saying people need to come and humble themselves on the floor right now."

I thought, "Okay, that's me." I jumped up to go to the front, but this time 50 kids responded as well. When I got to the front, I could feel that I was on the precipice of an encounter. I could feel God was just waiting for me to go full-face on the floor. This was the breaking point that He was waiting for. I said, "God, I give you everything!"

When I did that, the love that was pouring over me completely broke open and the trickle became a waterfall that went through my whole body. At that point, I saw my "old man" fly out of my body as this waterfall poured into me. And now I was having this experience of being born again. My spirit then left my body, and I could see the line of kids that had come up to the front as if I was floating over them. At this point, the speaker was going down the line praying for each one of the kids. The moment the encounter broke over me, I watched in my spirit as the speaker turned around and walked back over to me to prophesy.

To this day I don't know anything he spoke over me. He prophesied over me for a minute and when he left, I curled up in the fetal position weeping as the love of God poured over me. I was literally becoming a new creation. I don't know how long I was there, but in that moment I went into an open vision with my eyes closed.

In the vision, I was no longer in the fetal position but I was standing in a body of water. It was so big that I couldn't see the outer limits. There was so much peace and love in that moment that I was compelled to look over my right shoulder. Jesus was standing behind me on the bank of the water, and He looked at me and said, "What you are experiencing right now is My Presence," and He motioned to the body of water. There was so much peace and love in the moment that I was crying uncontrollably with snot, in the fetal position and quivering. I was experiencing the physical love of God and becoming a new creation in that moment. He then said to me, "You are experiencing My Presence, and you are only ankle deep."

When I looked down I realized I was only standing between ankle and calf deep in the water. He then said, "There is enough here for you to have as much as you want." I knew in that moment that what I was experiencing was just the beginning of a journey. As much as I was impacted, I realized I was only ankle deep! When He was done talking, a wave of life or energy came from Jesus through me. It was like my personal life commission became just knowing His Presence.

Then He said, "There is enough here (He motioned to the body of water) for anybody who has ever wanted any, to have as much as he wants." He gave me a peak into the reality of heaven; it was the reality of what God did for us. It is the opposite of the orphan spirit. There is enough for anybody who has ever wanted any to have as much as they want. When He motioned again, there was a second wave of energy from Him that went through me. It was as if my commission for ministry happened at the same time. Then the encounter was gone. I was back in my body in the fetal position on the floor. I would never be the same again.

The inner audible voice then said, "Find the kid from the first day that was trying to run away." I questioned God about whether He really wanted to interrupt the encounter I was having with Him. And He said again, "Get up and find that kid." It's not worth it to argue with God, so I got up, found the kid, and put my hand on his shoulder. I didn't have anything to say, but I was obedient to what God said to do. A second turned into a minute, and I began to feel an awkward tension. All of a sudden I could feel everything he was feeling and hear everything he was thinking. So I told him, "I can feel you wanting me to walk away from you right now, but more than that I can feel you not wanting me to walk away from you."

Out of nowhere, I started prophesying over his life about his past and about what he was called to do. He broke down crying. I had never prophesied before or heard anyone else prophesy, but it just happened. Then I started praying in tongues over him, but then reality set in. It was like I was sleep walking and had just woken up. I thought, "Oh my goodness. What am I doing?" The speaker grabbed the microphone and said, "Is there anybody out there that just needs a ministry team to come to you right now?" The reality hit me that I had no clue what I was doing. So I had the ministry team take over, and I went into the corner and just wept for another hour.

That was the start of my journey. It was an invitation into having as much of the Holy Ghost as I could ever want. I credit that day as marking me and setting me up for everything that has happened in my life and ministry since then. This encounter is the foundation of my message and the cornerstone of everything I've been going after for years: healing ministry, sonship, encounters, fullness, and all of these stem from this revelation and encounter.

Have your encounters increased since your first?
Yeah they've increased, but what I just shared was my foundation for increase. Something started when I said the "sinner's prayer," but I would

never say I was encountering Him. All of my encounters have come from the revelation, "I can have as much as I want." And of course there is a process that comes with that pursuit, but I always enter in through that belief.

With everyone coming from different backgrounds and experience levels with God, what advice would you give someone just beginning the process of encountering Him?
Know that Holy Spirit is a person. Spend a lot of time pursuing the presence. I have weeks of teaching on this stuff, but to sum it up—the Body of Christ is realizing and becoming more comfortable with the fact that Holy Spirit is a person, and He is as much a part of the Godhead as the Father and Son are. This is something the Church has known intellectually but not experientially. We all know the prayer, "Father, Son and Holy Spirit," but how many people actually take time to commune with Holy Spirit?

Do we pray to fellowship or worship Holy Spirit? Through false teaching there's been a fear of disillusionment brought into the Body of Christ. We have no fear to worship Jesus because we know that brings glory to the Father, but there has been fear to give as much attention to Holy Spirit.

We need to realize that they are one—that the Father, the Son, and the Holy Spirit are one in the same. That means you can't give glory or honor to one without giving glory to the others. When you worship Jesus, you are actually giving glory to the Father. The same is true with the Holy Spirit. You can't adore Holy Spirit or worship Him without at the same time bringing glory to the Father and the Son. In addition, the Holy Spirit is the part of the Godhead that is assigned to be on the earth and partner with the believer. So why wouldn't we give Him more time?

Not only are they equal, but the Holy Spirit is as much a part of the Godhead as Jesus or the Father. People in the church don't want to admit this openly. They just don't relate to Him as though He has equal portion. Holy Spirit is assigned to be with us on earth right now. John 16:13 says, "But when He, the Spirit of truth, comes, He will guide you into all the truth; for He will not speak on His own initiative, but whatever He hears, He will speak; and He will disclose to you what is to come."

People live under the lie that they are going to get distracted, off-track, or misled if they focus on Holy Spirit. But the Bible promises that Holy Spirit leads us into all truth, and Holy Spirit testifies of Jesus. If we want to grow in relationship with Jesus and Father, then our pursuit of a relationship with Holy Spirit is going to be the most direct path to that end.

The other thing I would tell people is to fall in love with the Presence. Even in revival circles, there is a belief that the Presence comes from the Father without recognizing that the Presence is Him. The Presence is God. It's not just an expression of God. When we feel the Presence of God come in the room—that is God Himself. Our limited awareness actually shortcuts what the Father wants to do in relationship, and it blinds us to the fact that God is literally coming in the room when we are worshiping or praying. We can all feel when the atmosphere in a room changes, when the peace comes in, when the little tingles come, and freedom enters. That's not a response to a good song; that is literally God Himself moving into the room.

But as long as we minimize His Presence to being something He does as an expression, then we are stuck still looking for something that is actually already here. When we begin to recognize that God just came in the room, our awe explodes in that moment and our encounters and our affection explode with it.

When we accomplish this we find ourselves having radical encounters without the effort we thought we needed to move into an encounter. Even in the culture of honor that we live in, where we get to receive the benefit of living in this place, I have never found anyone who responds to honor more than the Holy Spirit. You cannot honor Him and not have Him come. If you just start talking about Him in a loving way or start directing some of your praise and attention to Him, He will come!

Listen to Audio

THE HEARTBEAT OF MYSTICAL UNION
Geen George Varghese // Mystic // India

I love God more than anything else! Since I was a child or since I can remember, my biggest all-time hero has been God. I want to live a life for His pleasure, so walking in purity and holiness is really important to me. One day I prayed this prayer: "God, it would be better if I live just one day in purity and holiness and come home, than live a whole life without it. Please make me pure and holy!" Fire always falls on sacrifice.

A relationship has to live from expectation. I expect and need the activity of the Holy Spirit in my life all the time. God wants to encounter us because He is in love with us. But there is one really important thing: God gives us encounters just so we can encounter HIM. It's not so we can have more anointing, a large ministry, or knowledge—it is just because of Him.

When I read the Bible it is not just to get more knowledge about God, it is about a relationship. In my heart, I married Jesus. In my everyday life, the highest priority is the Holy Spirit. I want to honor Him. We can't command the Holy Spirit. He is sensitive, and we need to partner with Him and walk with Him as co-laborers. The Holy Spirit has really big dreams and visions, so we never need to push Him. His dreams and vision are much larger than ours.

My question to everyone is: How much do you want to have? Are you completely sure what it means to encounter Jesus? There is a big, life-changing cost. Also, expectation is a big thing. God will always give everyone as much they want and as much as they can handle.

HOW TO HEAR HIS VOICE
Francesco Sideli // Mystic // United States

The Scriptures that describe the relationship between Jesus and the Father have been so important to me during the past number of years. The Father loves the Son and shows Him all that He does. In the gospel of John, Jesus speaks about doing only what He sees the Father doing. My heart is so connected with that because it is all about a father and son relationship. It's about talking and dialogue, asking questions and getting answers. It's about removing stumbling blocks such as status, titles and privileges, and stripping all that down to the core relationship between a father and son.

What I like most about the prophetic is that it allows the Father to pursue me and allows me to respond to Him and ask Him questions. It allows God to creatively answer my question and allows me to enjoy His creativity in how He answers the questions. It is also similar to a relationship between a man and a woman as they pursue each other. I find this an exciting aspect of a relationship with God, it is a continual dance back and forth.

The Encounter
John 16:13 says, "The Holy Spirit will lead us into all truth." He will remind us of Jesus' words on a continual basis and He tells us what will happen in the future. He can also tell us what has happened in the past. I find this most enjoyable because I can ask Holy Spirit about a range of things in the future such as life transitions, information about upcoming events or natural events that will take place in anyone's life.

I remember going on a trip, and I asked the Lord, "What will take place during the trip?" He gave me some information on the first few days about what my role was to be with the group of people, what natural signs would occur as confirmation, as well as who will be discouraged at certain points

113

during the trip and what I would prophetically speak to them to encourage them. During the trip, there were some odd dynamics and a few of us encouraged a particular person. The questions I asked before the trip actually proved to be an important lifeline for that person.

During the whole trip, I was constantly asking the Father about what was going to happen. I would even prophesy encounters people would have and give team members detailed prophetic words about what was to come to pass. For example, I told one team member that she would go out during the day and heal a woman with a damaged knee. It happened just as I had prophesied. I was trying to become more specific in prophetic insight, so during the trip I gave another teammate a prophetic word and specific instructions. I shared that at 12:30 p.m. while evangelizing on the road, he should stop and look to the left in the crowd where he would see a man with a red cap. He remembered the prophecy, stopped, looked to his left and saw a man with a red hat, just as I had said.

How did your gift grow?

God is so faithful. Although I can't give a full theological explanation, I believe God places things in our hearts or He takes things that we have in our hearts and uses them to draw us into opportunities and situations. Some of my growth was just trial and error. Sometimes I have daydreams which God then reveals are not daydreams but actual events that will take place in the future.

For example, I was in a store with my wife just hanging out. I told her that I had to go to the rest room but would return quickly. On the way there, I had a daydream imagining myself coming back to her apologizing for taking a lot longer because I met a friend who I had not seen in a long time. I dismissed the daydream and continued to the elevator to get to the rest-room. Suddenly one of my friends who I have not seen for a while came by. He was there to see his wife who worked on a lower floor. We began talking for a while. He told me that he was about to leave and asked if I would come with him downstairs to continue talking a little more. After that I went back upstairs to my wife and began to apologize to her for being longer than expected. I immediately realized that the vision that I had seen earlier was an accurate foreshadow of what took place!

These experiences are great because this is an indication that God is having a dialogue with me. This begs the question: if He dialogues with me on this matter, what else would He discuss?

On another occasion, I received prophetic words about natural events that would take place in a certain country. I went to a conference there, shared the prophecy and gave them an explanation of what God was doing through the natural events. A few months later, the natural events took place and the people remembered what I told them God was going to do.

Another example of learning to grow deeper in my dialogue with God is that at the beginning of the day I might ask Him, "When I go to school what will a certain person be wearing?" I could go deeper and ask, "What can I pray for this person?" God will tell me what to pray. I could go even deeper by asking what is God's heart for the person and how could I encourage them. And God will give specific instructions. Or I might ask questions about an institution and for God to reveal His heart for that place. I usually ask for specifics, so He can be glorified when they are revealed. The questions can always get deeper; we can seek God's heart in every way.

God responds in a variety of creative ways such as thoughts, voice, visions, and dreams. Sometimes I see numbers reoccurring, see certain natural events take place, or three people will come into a store with pain in the same area. So, I am always asking the Lord for meaning to the signs I see.

How is this applied in different venues other than the church?
Recently, I spoke to a group of business people and prophesied over some of them. Sometimes I ask the Lord specific questions when the situation warrants it in order to address a particular need. Sometimes, I try to find areas that I want the Lord to pinpoint.

For example, a businessman was traveling here, and the Lord said to me "cancer." I then asked the Lord, "Why cancer?" He told me that He was giving this man a particular authority over cancer. I didn't leave it at that, but I went even deeper with my questions. I then asked, "Why?" and He told me that cancer has been in his family. I asked where cancer was in the man's family and God revealed that it was on his father's side—that both his father and grandfather had cancer. I used this knowledge to prophesy over the businessman. He was really appreciative, since, he later expressed fear of contracting the illness himself.

A more fitting example would be when I was ministering to a man, and I asked the Lord what his prayer request was and what the answer was that He wanted to give him in reply. The Lord outlined the man's prayer and His answer to the prayer during that particular season. I then told the man everything the Lord had said, and he was deeply moved and appreciative.

Also at the beginning of the day, I ask the Holy Spirit details about my day. One time He told me that I would see a Ford minivan on a certain street. When I got to the street, the van was there and the Lord told me that He did this because of His love for me. I celebrated that. As I went a little further, I asked the Lord to reveal more and He brought a person to mind. He told me their prayer request, what was happening in their life and gave me a prophetic word for them. I enjoy this moment-by-moment relationship with the Father, seeking answers to questions.

It is important to stretch and grow our capacities in hearing God. I want to grow continuously. This desire might be linked to my Italian heritage; my family really likes talking about things in detail. In the same way, I enjoy this aspect of talking with the Lord. I try to be specific in my prophetic words.

One time I wanted to encourage a lady, so I told her that she would receive a particular Bible verse from Jeremiah within a week that would greatly encourage her. She acknowledged the prophecy and looked forward to receiving it. But after a week nothing happened; she got nothing at all. Consequently I apologized to her since I thought I received God's message wrongly—it's good to take ownership for mistakes as well. Approximately three weeks later, she told me that she got an encouraging verse from the book of Jeremiah, which was needed at that time. When God gave me the initial prophetic word I may have been presumptuous or excited and did not take care to make sure I had all the right details.

Sometimes, I will see something in the spirit, but seeing is only part of it. I've had to learn not to make assumptions about the rest. This happened to me recently when I told God that I was going to the gas station. He told me that I will see a woman by the pump placing gas in a black Ford and nearby would be a white SUV facing the road. When I went to the gas station, I saw the white SUV at the location and a lady pumping gas into a Ford car. However, the car was not black, but she was wearing a black dress. This is an illustration of how at times I do not accurately have all the details.

Another example is when I went to a parking lot, and I asked God on the way if there was something He wanted me to do. He told me to pray for a woman with a certain color car. When I got to the location, I saw not just one, but a number of cars in similar colors with female drivers. Then I realized that I should have asked more questions. You can never have too many details!

I believe that God doesn't always give us all the details in an effort to get us to go deeper with Him. One of these ways is by asking further questions and looking forward to His response. He is looking for a relationship. Through dialogue we grow closer in our relationship. Through this dialogue our faith increases. My relationship with God has grown to where I no longer have to initiate the communication with God, but He also initiates and shares His secrets with me. It's very important to me to have a two-way relationship where God comes to me, not just me coming to Him. I love and rejoice in this relationship with God!

THE PROCESS
Steve Moore // Mystic // United States

I grew up in a Christian home and went to a Baptist Church, so there was no understanding of the supernatural or of the theology that the gifts of the Spirit are for today. I grew up with a very religious background, except that my parents were very gracious, and my mom always talked about how God can do anything. My mom had supernatural encounters as a child, and she told stories of these encounters. So I knew the supernatural was possible because I had the understanding that God could do whatever He wanted. At the same time I didn't have the revelation or the awareness that I could actually experience it for myself. It was more the mentality that it was a "sovereign move of God" on my mom's life.

Growing up I was a Christian, and I was really into playing sports. I was looking to play college ball, but I got hurt my senior year in high school. When I went to college, I drifted away from the Lord for a bit because I got a little bitter and upset about my injury preventing me from my desire to play sports in college.

So, I got into the party scene and drinking. While I was away, my mom started calling me to tell me that she was praying for people on the streets, and they were getting healed. My mom had believed her whole life that if she would pray for people they would get healed. One of her heroes was Smith Wigglesworth. And when she would read about him healing people, she just believed that she could too. She would call me to tell me all the testimonies she was experiencing. Even though I had walked away from God, I believed her because she is one of the most integrous people I know. She kept telling me, "Steve you can do it too. You have access too. All you have to do is just believe." She started talking to me about just believing, and I actually started to step out and pray for people.

The first person I prayed for was a football player. He had a torn back muscle and was supposed to be out for nine weeks. I saw him on the streets and asked him if I could pray for him. He agreed thinking I could pray for him another time, but I asked if we could pray right then and there.

The first seven times I prayed, nothing happened. After each time, I kept asking if I could pray again. My mom had told me, "Steve, it will happen through you. All you have to do is just believe." After the seventh prayer when it didn't happen, I was so mad. I said, "Dude, let me pray one more time and I promise you, you're going to get healed," I was thinking that what my mom told me has to be true because she is not a liar, and the Word is not a liar, so this had to be true. I prayed for him one last time, and as soon as I said one word, his back muscle grew out underneath my hand. The guy was instantly healed and cleared two days later to play football again even though he was supposed to be out for a while.

When that happened I was still going to parties. I was getting drunk, praying for people at parties and they were getting healed. I am definitely not endorsing that behavior by any means. But it was a testimony of God's grace, His goodness, and the power of faith and belief.

Shortly after that experience, I had an encounter at a Jesus Culture event that I didn't want to go to. My mom had encouraged my whole family who got set on fire because of her testimonies. My 88 year-old grandpa was chasing people on crutches on the streets to pray for them. He called me to tell me that he bought me a ticket for a Jesus Culture event happening that weekend. I didn't want to go, but I figured I would honor him and go anyway. The night before I had a bunch of beers, so I drove to the event hung over.

Since I was hung over I really didn't want to be there, but in the middle of Banning Liebscher's preaching, he stopped and said, "There is someone here with a sports injury. You keep dislocating your shoulder, and you don't know why but doctors have tried to fix it. Why don't you stand up?" That was me—I had dislocated my shoulder 24 times with all these torn ligaments and nothing was working to fix it, even surgery. So I stood up.

I was the only one standing out of 1600 people. As soon I stood up, nobody laid hands on me, but the fire of God hit me. My whole body felt engulfed with fire. I felt something in my shoulder moving around, and I was having a crazy powerful encounter with His love and goodness. From that moment on, not only did my hang over leave instantly, but my shoulder was healed, and I was delivered.

When I came home my friends wondered what happened to me. These were fraternity guys who were not walking with the Lord, but they noticed something was different about me. From that point on, I didn't have a desire to drink or get drunk. I just wanted to pursue His Presence and His goodness. I began seeking God and understanding that we already have access to Him because of the cross. We have full access to everything because of what Jesus purchased. God started taking me through Scripture and showed me how finished the work of the cross really was. He showed me how much access we have, that we really are sons, and we get to have a relationship with a God who speaks. I started getting words of knowledge for people because I was in this close relationship with God. He was in me, and I was in Him.

I had a revelation about 1 Corinthians 2:16 that says we have the mind of Christ. He started talking to me saying, "Steve, when your thoughts are focused on communing with Me then your thoughts become like mine. And I'll start showing up in your thoughts." I just started having impressions about people that I began to share with them. They would confirm that my impressions were true.

I've really been on a journey of taking risk and stepping out. I didn't have anyone teaching me about this other than what my mom had shared with me. I was learning that God is not distant but actually one with me. I started realizing that the God of the universe lives inside of me, fully consuming me. When that finally clicked, everything started changing. If He's inside of me, then that means I can encounter Him whenever I want. And when I started putting faith with that, I started to have more encounters with him.

I've never been the same since.

JESUS IS MY EVERYTHING
Lauren DeTombe // MDCM Anthology Team // United States

The Process

When I was about 15, I encountered God really powerfully and came to the realization there was a call on my life. I totally changed my course. I was very broken at the time and living in a stressful home situation. I began spending hours by myself journaling, worshiping and reading the Bible. Often I would fall asleep on my face with music on.

I would read all kinds of old books about revivalists and missionaries, and I began to feast on their encounters and walks with the Lord. God began to do lots of inner healing in me. He would tell me to put on a song, and I knew part of me would be healed. I would weep for 30 minutes and get up changed. His presence would get so heavy in my room as I worshiped that sometimes I just wouldn't get up. I got baptized in the Holy Spirit when I was 16, and I really began to encounter more supernatural things after that. Sometimes, I felt I was entertaining Jesus in my room and could even tell you where He was in the room. During these times I would dance for Him.

For the most part, my mentors were books written by Benny Hinn, Jackie Pullinger, Mahesh Chavda, Maria Woodworth Etter, Todd Bentley and many more missionaries. I began to let things happen to me that God was doing, and I slowly started to allow Him to encounter me however He wanted. I spent hours with the Lord and did crazy prophetic acts.

To try and strengthen my reliance on the Holy Spirit, I once tried to walk around the perimeter of my house blindfolded, which was a big compound. My hunger to know the Lord became like a matter of life and death. Holy Spirit has been the closest friend to me. Only this year have I ever thought I could be a mystic. I am definitely a beginner in the ways of the Spirit and have a lot to learn. I don't really care about having a title. I only care about knowing Jesus and being known by Him. It's all part of a relationship with Jesus... how real is He to you? Jesus is a person and the "unseen" realm is more real than what we can see.

The Encounter

I was feeling really overwhelmed and like I was failing. In that moment, I was reminded of what God had told me recently. He said that the angels by the throne knew my name and there was a well-worn path to the throne that I had cultivated. I was trying to encourage myself and remind myself to keep being diligent.

"I was being held tightly by Jesus even as He was running. I could feel His heart thumping fast and the movement as He ran."

As soon as I was reminded of the path to the throne, Jesus said, "Most of the time I was the One carrying you there." All of a sudden, I felt like I was pressed up against a big chest. I was being held tightly by Jesus even as He was running. I could feel His heart thumping fast and the movement as He ran. I could sense this incredible urgency unlike anything I had felt before. Jesus was running down the path to His Father's throne. I could almost feel His tears or sweat falling on my face. I felt really safe and also like I was being crushed in His arms.

At one point while Jesus was running, He began to do mouth to mouth resuscitation. I felt as if someone was breathing into me. He was saying, "I'm not letting one part of you die! All of you has to make it." He was like an EMT. He rushed me to the throne, and it was the first time I had ever experienced both Jesus and Father God in interaction with one another.

Jesus ran to the throne and looked at the Father and said, "Here take her. Help her Father. She needs you."

He was interceding for me and lying before His Father's throne. I could feel the overwhelming passion Jesus had for me and the honor He had for His Father. I had never realized before that Jesus was passionate about bringing me before His Father. Jesus and the Father ministered to me so powerfully. I got up from that encounter after having wept harder than I had in a long time. I was never to be the same again.

Teresa of Avila
(ca. 1315 – 1382)

"There are more tears shed over answered prayers than over
unanswered prayers."

"You pay God a compliment by asking great things of Him."

Teresa of Avila was a medieval nun and mystic whose scholarly work gave
her the distinction as a "doctor of the church." She was born into a Jewish
family and entered the Catholic Carmelite order around 1535. It was not
until twenty years later that she experienced a conversion to the higher state
of contemplative prayer.

At that stage, Christ appeared to her and said, "Do not be distressed, for I
will give you a living book." He then began to grant her visions and
experiences of union that moved her to write the account of her inner life
known as "Vida" or "Life". For Teresa of Avila, progress in prayer is
synonymous with a deepening union with God. She describes this process in
a section of "Vida" as the four degrees of prayer.

In her book "Vida," Teresa also describes an ecstatic vision of the piercing
of her heart, which took place around 1560. Here is a short excerpt: "I saw
an angel close to me, on my left side, in bodily form... I saw in his hand a
long spear of gold, and at the iron's point there seemed to be a little fire...
the pain (from the sword) was so great that it made me moan; and yet so
surpassing was the sweetness of this excessive pain that I could not wish to
be rid of it."

For Teresa, union with God was a tangible experience that demanded to be felt and enjoyed by all one's senses and emotions. Her process of knowing God became her way of life. Her relationship with God was not a daily discipline but more a personal journey of getting to know a friend. Simply, God was not left on the pages of the Bible, but He was invited into to all aspects of her life.

The Process from a Biblical Perspective

Compare no man to another. In Galatians 6:4, Paul states that, "Each one should test their own actions. Then they can take pride in themselves alone, without comparing themselves to someone else." The process of walking out the call of God for one individual might be different from another. For instance, David started giant killing as a teenager and was in pursuit of God from an even younger age. Yet, Moses didn't even begin walking in his calling until 80 years of age. God spoke to Daniel and Jacob through dreams, but there is not a single recorded instance of Jesus, the Son of God, having a dream in the Bible.

In these Biblical instances, we know that God did not favor Daniel or Jacob over Jesus, yet why did they get dreams and Jesus didn't? Or why did Enoch and Elijah get to be taken up to heaven before their time, yet Peter and many of the other New Testament apostles were martyred in very brutal ways? As a matter of fact, there was not a single Old Testament martyr, outside of Samson, yet most of the New Testament apostles were martyrs. Are the Old Testament followers of God more favored than those of the New Testament?

Jesus actually rebuked Peter for this type of comparison thinking. At the end of John 21, Jesus told the disciples about what kind of death they would have to suffer for following Him. After this Peter turned to Jesus and asked about John who wasn't included in the conversation. Jesus replied, "If I want Him to remain until I come, what is that to you? You follow me!"

Another story that illustrates the difference in one's process can be found in Mark 5 when Jesus was met by Jairus, a synagogue official. He was a man that had spent most of his life pursuing God, so when his daughter died he went to Jesus for healing. While Jesus was on the way to his house a woman touched Him and was healed. In contrast, this woman had spent everything she had for 12 years trying to get healed by the best physicians. In one case, a man had pursued God his whole life, and in the other, from what we can tell, the woman had spent a good portion of her life pursuing the world's answers to her problem. Yet, when they both came to Jesus, they both were healed. Each had extremely different processes of coming to Christ, nonetheless when they met Him they both received the same reward.

So whether it is your process of getting healed, learning your authority in Christ or walking out your call in God, everyone's journey looks different. Some begin with faith but fade into fear, while others begin in fear but fall into His faith. What the process looks like doesn't matter. In the end, we should take Jesus' advice to Peter, "What is that to you? You follow me!"

TRANSPORTATIONS

TRANSPORTATION IS FUN
Jason Smedley // Mystic // United States

My journey into the mystery realm has been a strange one. I was born with a profound gift to relate to the spirit world. Having Jesus physically appear to you at 2 years old and give you valid medical advice for someone else isn't your typical childhood experience. I've had strange events happen my entire life, but I never really thought it was anything special because I thought everyone had these kinds of experiences. It wasn't until after I turned 20 that I began to realize that other people didn't have these same experiences.

To be honest, I don't like the word "mystic." Maybe it's because it's popular to be a mystic right now, and I'm not into following trends; I'm not sure. But the truth is I fit the description. Something that is equally true is that I never really feel like a mystic. An important aspect of my journey as a mystic is realizing I am one even though I don't feel like it. The biggest trap I've seen others fall into is based on this; they don't feel like a mystic so they boast to try and prove that they are. The fact is that my calling is real and not just an illusion of grandeur. Resting in that fact, instead of striving to prove it, has been a huge aid in my journey of becoming who I am today.

That being said, I've been asked to share some mystical experiences that I've had. These are not my "greatest" encounters, but I believe there is an important lesson in them. The first one happened to me around Christmas in 2012. I have a tendency to leave my body and travel places. I don't mean I close my eyes and imagine myself going places. I mean I literally have an out of body experience, and it feels more real than physical reality. In this experience, I was outside of my body and found myself among two angels. To the left of one of the angels was a doorway that I felt led to go through. Once on the other side, I instantly found myself in my parent's house in Los Angeles, CA. As I walked through their house, I ran into the spirit of my parent's dog "Desi" (she had died recently). I understand the "theological hairs" this story raises, but I'm simply sharing what happened. As I watched, the Lord told me He brought me there to confirm to my parents that Desi's spirit was indeed walking through their house, and it wasn't a psychological trick their minds were playing on them. Then toward the end of the experience, I heard a voice invite Desi to come jump up onto their bed.

A day later I called my mom to share what had happened. After I shared with her, she gasped in sudden shock! She told me that the same exact night I had my encounter, the Lord woke her up and told her that He was allowing Desi to come and walk through their house. After that she looked and saw her dead dog jump up onto their bed! Because she was unsure about the experience she prayed and said, "Lord, please let me know this was you and not just a psychological hallucination. Please, if this was you, give me a sign. Would you confirm it through someone who could have no idea about what just happened? Would you confirm it through Jason?"

Needless to say she was in shock when I told her what I had witnessed! To be honest, it seems to me that God used a pretty high level mystical experience on a pretty unimportant situation. Take me out of my body and travel through a portal— all over a dead dog?! Really God?!

Another quick dog related miracle that happened during this last Christmas in 2013 (oddly enough!) was that my niece fed a dog a whole container of lip-gloss! By the time I grabbed it from her, it was totally empty with bite marks along the sides. I showed my sister and she was upset. We put the lid on and set it on the counter. An hour later, she opened it again, and it was completely full!

God is so jealous for our mindsets that many of the miracles He performs seem trivial. But they are heat-seeking missiles designed to destroy unbelief and lead us into one of the greatest miracles of all: a transformed mind!

This shows me that the little things in our lives that seem unimportant are incredibly important to Him. He places importance, urgency, and value on things much differently than we do. It compels me to want to exchange my value system for His. Heaven's perspective is so much different than earth's. Sometimes a paradigm shift is more important to God than other things we deem urgent.

DESTROYING THE WORKS OF DARKNESS
Slindile Baloyi // Mystic // South Africa

Over the years, I've been on a journey of experimenting with travelling in the spirit realm. In the Bible, there are a few examples of people who traveled in the spirit realm. Jesus was one of them, and I wanted to have that same experience manifest in my life.

The unseen realm of the spirit is real and available to every believer. One of the gifts that Holy Spirit has given us is the discernment between spirits. We do this by first recognizing that we are spirit beings, and that a lot of the affliction and intimidation happening to people is rooted in some kind of spirit. Some examples of these spirits are fear, rejection, anger, and suicide. They manifest on a person through afflicting their mind, body or soul.

In the great commission, Jesus said, "All authority in heaven and on earth has been given to Me, therefore go make disciples of all nations." We destroy the works of the devil by believing that Jesus living in us is enough to give us dominion over principalities and the "spirit of this age." We as the body of Christ must recognize that our fight is not against flesh and blood but against principalities that build themselves up against the knowledge of God.

Together with Holy Spirit, I love to travel in my spirit to dark places and actually set people free. So every night before I go to bed, I speak to my spirit and bless it to travel anywhere it desires. Below is an example of one of those experiences.

One night as I lay asleep, I heard a voice in my spirit asking me, "So are you ready?" I immediately responded, "YES." Suddenly I saw my spirit come out from my body. It was like a bright white light coming out of my stomach. We shot straight up into the sky in the direction of Heaven. With great speed I went though what first seemed like tunnels that were spiraling upward and at the same time, I could see myself going through galaxies.

I had traveled to heaven many times before, but this was different. My spirit was literally leading me, and yet somehow it felt like I was in partnership together with the Holy Spirit. As we kept flying higher, I suddenly had this thought, "Wait, I have been to heaven many times, can we go down below to where Sheol is—where demons rule from instead?" Immediately we changed directions, and we were flying back toward earth in what felt like the speed of light.

"I crouched amidst the demons, and could see them (there were many of them). Somehow my spirit shielded me so that they couldn't see me. It was like a cloak was over me."

As we came closer to underneath the earth, I began to feel, see and smell all kinds of spirits in the atmosphere—fear, anxiety, a foul smell, heaviness, intimidation, etc. At some point we stopped at what looked like a place where the enemy meets to strategize on how to destroy earth. I crouched amidst the demons, and could see them (there were many of them). Somehow my spirit shielded me so that they couldn't see me. It was like a cloak was over me. At some point, one of the principalities of darkness looked directly in my direction, and then walked away. The underground was filled with distorted looking "people." More accurately, they were demons who looked like people that were filthy, creepy looking, etc.

When I went closer to hear what was being planned, I heard about a cargo container in Indonesia full of women and children about to be shipped for sex trafficking. In an instant, I found myself on a dock, and I knew I was in Indonesia in my physical body. I knew exactly what color this cargo container was, where it was located, and even knew how to unlock it. I knew this instinctively in my spirit. As I opened the cargo container, I saw tons of eyes looking back at me. There were women and children who had been cramped in darkness for a couple days and were very afraid.

With one finger on my mouth to signal silence, I motioned to them with my other hand to follow me out of the container. We had to be very careful, as there were two guards with guns guarding this container. Our footsteps could have alerted the guards. One by one they jumped out of the container and began to follow me. As we were doing this, I was aware of the danger but felt total peace. Somehow I knew I was covered by Holy Spirit.

Next we came to what looked like an underground bridge with a tunnel, and I could see light on the other side. I knew that this bridge was the place where you could cross over to the other side of town for safety. As we began to walk under the bridge toward the light, I suddenly came back into my body and was lying on my bed. My heart was beating super fast from all the excitement and awareness of my rescue mission. I had just done something huge for the kingdom—I destroyed the plans of the enemy by traveling in my spirit and had taken the risk to go into an area that was heavily guarded. My intention was to save those women and children, and I fully succeeded.

Sometime later I shared this story to a lady I met here in Redding who was from Indonesia. As I shared this story with her, the Spirit of God fell on her, and she began to weep. She then told me afterward that she has always known that it's possible to stop the sex trafficking trade in her country but didn't know how to do it. My story helped her realize that she could do this in the spirit realm. It set her on a journey to grow in understanding traveling in the spirit realm. I believe my words gave her grace to step into something greater.

I share this story to encourage all believers that part of our inheritance in Christ is to travel in the spirit. We can travel to nations, to heaven, to see the things of God and to encounter Him. But we also have the ability by the Holy Spirit to travel to the enemy's camp and to destroy his plans.

I learned through this travel experience that even though I felt intense spirits of fear, anxiety, intimidation, I was more aware of the Life of Christ in me and His commission to destroy the works of the devil. I love doing this because I know it gives the Father pleasure.

FOOD IS IMPORTANT
Jason Chin // Mystic // United States

On the way home from a ministry trip in Los Angeles, California, we stopped at a gas station to rest and get some gas. One of the team members, Jonathan, had lost his turkey and cheese Lunchable, so a bunch of us began looking for it. We couldn't find it after searching for a while, so we gave up. Right before we were about to leave one of the students said, "Why don't we just transport back to Redding, California so we don't have to drive?" The eight of us gathered into a circle, grabbed hands, and said, "By faith we can transport back to Redding."

Immediately we all felt a shift and someone shouted, "Let's go to our church." Then some of the students started seeing the prayer house in the spirit and by faith we stepped into it and started looking around. When we were done every person on the team had seem the same vision of a lady with a blue shirt, shorts, and brown hair who was waving a flag as she prayed. We were so convinced that it was real that we started calling people that could go to the prayer house to confirm what we saw. When we finished the encounter, Jonathan started freaking out. We turned to look at him and his turkey and cheese Lunchable was now in his hand!

We were trying to be transported. We wanted to step into that realm with God. Although we weren't physically transported, we all saw the same vision, and more importantly, Jonathan's Lunchable physically appeared in his hand! In a way it was a "first fruits" experience. It was God's way of telling us that we were moving in the right direction. I feel like He was playing a joke with us and just wanting to have fun.

Another example of this was when the Lord was talking to me about the number "10." He was saying, "Jason, the number 10 is important for your life. I want you to read Matthew, Mark, Luke, John, Acts, and Romans chapters 10." When I read them they were all about Jesus commissioning the 12 or 72 disciples or Romans 10: "How will they know the good news unless somebody actually tells them," and Acts 10:38, "God anointed Him (Jesus) with the Holy Spirit and with power, and He went about doing good and healing all who were oppressed by the devil, for God was with Him."

I was at my desk with my eyes closed as God was speaking these things to me. When I opened my eyes there was a brand new 10 dollar bill that had materialized on my desk. I picked up the ten dollar bill and saw that the serial number was my birthday and the very first prophecy I ever received was stamped on the bill. It was a season where God would speak to me but then confirm it in the natural. God wants to be interacted with. It's time we started treating Him as if He is truly with us!

John G. Lake
(ca. 1870 – 1935)

John G. Lake was born into a family of 15 with 8 of his siblings dying at a young age. This constant state of death and disease in his family led him to bring this heartache to the Lord. In this pursuit, he learned that sickness and disease were not from God, but they were from the devil. This instilled in him a deep detestation for death. With this newfound understanding many of his remaining family members, including his wife, began getting healed from being bedridden and many other sicknesses. The word spread, and Mr. Lake began an international healing ministry.

Along with healing hundreds of thousands of people worldwide, many other miracles followed Lake and his ministry. One of these miracles took place during a Sunday service when Lake and the audience began praying for an individual's cousin who was mentally ill and therefore required to live in an institution.

As the spirit of prayer fell on the congregation, Lake described the event in this way: "I seemed out of the body, and to my surprise observed that I was rapidly passing over the city of Kimberly, three hundred miles from Johannesburg. The next consciousness was the city of Cape Town, on the seacoast, one thousand miles away. The next consciousness was the island of St. Helena where Napoleon was banished. Then the Cape Verde lighthouse on the coast of Spain came into view. By this time it seemed as if I was passing with great lightning-like rapidity... Presently a village appeared, nestled in a deep valley among the hills[1]."

To make a long story short, in addition, during this experience he visited France, North Dakota, Wales and so on, all in this one experience of transportation. Finally, he arrived in a village in Wales, which he described in great detail, including the door and the building he entered. At that time, he saw a woman strapped to a bed who was muttering incoherently. She was undoubtedly demon possessed. When he laid his hands upon her, he commanded the spirit to leave. In a moment, the women's countenance softened, her eyes opened and she smiled.

When it was all over, he opened his eyes and found himself kneeling in prayer as if he had never left. Three weeks later a member from the congregation came up to him asking for prayer with a letter from one of his relatives saying, "An unusual thing had occurred. Their cousin, who had been confined for seven years in an asylum in Wales, suddenly became well." The doctors had no explanation of what happened, and the woman returned to her friends and family perfectly healthy.

1   Kenneth Copeland, "John G. Lake-- His Life, His Sermons, His Boldness of Faith," pgs 245, 246. Kenneth Copeland Publications 1994.

Ezekiel
(bc. 622 - 570)

Ezekiel was one of the 3000 Jews exiled to Babylon by King Nebuchadnezzar in 597 B.C. During this time Ezekiel performed some of the oddest prophetic acts recorded in the Bible. For example, he lived on his side for over a year, only eating bread cooked over animal dung as a prophetic act. He was a man that recklessly gave his life to God and walked uprightly during a time when few others were. He is considered a "major" prophet in the Old Testament and has more dates and details attached to his prophesies than any other prophet in the Bible, which makes his prophesies some of the easiest to judge.

In several instances, the Lord actually physically moves Ezekiel by His Spirit. In Ezekiel 3, the Lord lifted him up and transported him to the river of Chebar for 7 days. Another time in Ezekiel 37, the Spirit transported him to the valley of dry bones to prophesy. In two other instances (Ezekiel 2:2 and 3:24), the Spirit physically entered Ezekiel and lifted him to his feet before he even had a chance to obey.

These stories along with many others in the Bible beautifully display how connected the spiritual and physical realms are. As in the case of Ezekiel, whether he was moved to the heavens or places on the earth, the Spirit was a tangible part of his life and walk with God. The Spirit of God physically affects the natural world. It was never meant for there to be a loose relationship between the two, back then or now.

VISIONS

CHARIOTS OF FIRE // MANTLE OF ELIJAH
Joaquin Evans // Mystic // United States

About five years ago, a team from my church went to Israel to help with a youth conference. We had a radical time seeing tons of miracles and other amazing encounters. Israel is wide open for God to move. One particular night we were ministering in Jerusalem and had just finished an evening meeting, so we took off on a couple-hour drive through the night to Mount Carmel.

As we were driving on a freeway, the car we were following whipped across two lanes of traffic and took an exit. My legs started to vibrate, which happens a lot when I'm about to enter an encounter. This time was different because I was driving a car, not worshiping or laying on the floor soaking… but it felt like I was in the encounter realm. When I looked up, I saw a pillar of fire come down on the mountain. Then Joshua Stevens who was in the passenger seat yelled, "Oh my goodness, there is a pillar of fire!" He pointed out what I saw before I even had a chance to tell the others in the car. At that moment, the presence of God exploded in the car.

We all begin shaking, flopping, and vibrating violently. Then the lead car flipped another U-turn and headed back toward the freeway. I didn't know why we were heading this direction or why we had just turned around. All I knew is that we were now headed in the wrong direction away from this encounter with God. We didn't know where we were and didn't want to get lost, so we made the U-turn to follow the car. At this point, everyone in our car was saying, "NO! NO! We are going in the wrong direction." So we called out to God, "We don't know why we are going the wrong direction now. We don't know what's happening, but don't let us miss what You have for us!"

146

Just as we said this, flaming horses came out of the pillar of fire and began to chase our car. Again, before I could even say anything, Kris Kildosher yelled out, "Oh my gosh, there are flaming hoses and chariots chasing our car!" When they reached the car, the presence of God exploded in the car. I almost blacked out, and my head hit the driver side window. I was driving one-handed, but somehow we got back on the freeway. We drove another 30 minutes, with my head still on the window as we were being destroyed by this thick presence of God. The fear and awe of God had truly filled the car. When we finally pulled up to a gas station, we were stuck in the car under a thick presence.

One of the girls we were following came to see what was going on in our car, and the presence of God hit her so hard she fell out over my lap and into the car. All the other girls ran up to see what was going on. When they got within a few feet of the car, they all fell out under the Spirit of God as well. A cloud filled the car to the point that the windows fogged out, even with all four of the doors wide open. This went on for about 20 minutes.

Then some drag racers pulled their cars into the parking lot. Long story short, a bunch of the guys got healed and a lot of prophetic words started flowing for about an hour. When we finally arrived to where we were going that night, I asked the lady driving the lead car what had happened. She then told me that she felt two hands grab her hands and yank the steering wheel. She said, "I didn't know what happened. And I didn't know what else to do, so I just made a u-turn to get back to the freeway."

I told her we had to find that exit again. The next day we went back to Jerusalem where we were the night before. We found out that the exit we swerved to follow was the southern most point of the Carmel mountain range. We really wanted to get to the top of the mountain. The only problem was that the entire mountain was surrounded by villages with no clear-cut roads or street signs. We tried three times to get to the top using our best guesses and rationale. Then we decided to try following His presence. When we did it that way, we made it to the top without one wrong turn!

"Finally the Spirit of God hit me, and I went into an open vision. A scroll came down and God highlighted many verses of the Bible."

When we reached the top of the mountain, we spent about 45 minutes just praying fervently about what happened the night before. Finally the Spirit of God hit me, and I went into an open vision. A scroll came down and God highlighted many verses of the Bible. He showed me Elijah and the battle with the Baal Prophets on top of Mt. Carmel, and the pillar of fire that came down on the mountain to consume the prophets. Then it transitioned to the time when Elisha followed Elijah to get a double portion of his anointing, where flaming horses and chariots came down, and Elijah was taken up in a whirlwind.

I know a lot of teaching focuses on how the horses and chariots were a distraction to test Elisha to see if he would watch Elijah, but that teaching never sat well with me. In the vision I was having, I saw the horses and chariots' come down and Elisha cried out, "My father, my father the horseman and the chariots of Israel!" Then at that moment, something hit my spirit as the Lord said to me, "The horses and chariots were the spiritual representation of Elijah's office. The cloak that fell afterwards was the physical representation of the mantle that went with the office." Elisha was supposed to keep his eyes on Elijah, but his heart cry was "My father, my father the horseman and the chariots of Israel." If they were a distraction, why would that be his response? He actually recognized the mantle.

The scene switched a couple more times from the exchange between Elisha and his servant, to Malachi explaining the restoration of the fathers to their sons through Elijah, and lastly to Jesus (in Mark 9) explaining how the spirit of Elijah has come for the restoration of all things.

All of this happened in about 30 seconds, and when the scroll disappeared, a fear hit me like I can't explain. It was the "Fear of the Lord." In that moment, I started to understand what I had seen. For a millisecond I wondered if that mantle was being transferred onto me. But the Lord quickly responded by telling me it wasn't for me, but that He was giving me a glimpse of what He is releasing on a generation.

God is releasing a promise that a whole generation is coming into agreement with that mantle of Elijah, which is for the restoration of all things—families, governments, and physical healing. There is no limit to what He wants to release for those who pursue Him and His presence. Then the Lord said that a new measure came upon me, but He reminded me it's not just for me, but it's for a generation. He also said spirits would be sent to partner with me to accomplish this. When He said that, a whole corral of horses came up to me in the spirit, and the Lord told me to take time to get to know the characteristics and nature of the mantle. Then they were gone. I walked back to the car— I was undone.

Colossians 1:19-20 says, "For it pleased the Father that in Him (Jesus) the fullness should dwell and by Him, He should reconcile all things..." It actually pleases the Father to restore all things. Unfortunately, when some believers read in the Scriptures, "to please the Father" they actually think in their heart that we have to "appease" Him. They think it means to keep Him happy, to keep Him at bay or to keep Him pacified. With this comes the mentality that we have to do what He is saying or He'll be upset with us. But that's not what it's saying. "I no longer call you slaves (John 15:15)..." It **pleases** the Father, not appeases Him, but brings Him pleasure to restore all things to the way they were in the garden. He loves to restore things to the way they were in the garden before sin was ever in the picture.

God is actually releasing this anointing for restoration of all things to anyone who pursues His presence. Anyone who will dive into who He is and partner with His pleasure has the ability to see things restored. There is a radical increase coming on the body of Christ. There is power and authority to see the promises of God fulfilled. This wave is the beginning of seeing all things restored. This is to bring us to the place where we realize, "I have a right to see cancer eradicated from bodies or broken bones healed!" There is still so much more to see.

Listen to audio

LET THE ADVENTURE BEGIN
Andrea Hoheisel // Mystic // United States

I was in worship at church, and as I stood there singing, Jesus walked up to me. He had a baby in His arms that He reached out to hand me, and then He asked me to nurse it. I shook my head and said, "No, Lord it's not mine." I could see the mother standing right behind Jesus. I knew it was her baby and not mine. Again Jesus stretched out His arms to hand me the baby, which was wrapped in a blanket. I repeated, "No, Lord. It's not mine. I can see the mother right behind you."

Jesus looked over His shoulder to where the woman was standing. In silent communication the woman looked at Him and then to me. She nodded at me and smiled. I took this to mean it was what she wanted also. As Jesus held out His arms once again asking me to take this baby and nurse it, I took the baby and immediately began nursing it. Instantly, the woman was gone, and I looked to see Jesus smiling at me before He disappeared. At that moment I realised that I was still in worship. It felt like this encounter lasted for a while, but only moments had passed. As I asked the Lord what this meant, I felt Him saying that I would care for those that were not my own and nurse or bring life to those needing nourishment.

On another occasion, as I was spending time with the Lord, I was taken into a vision. I was standing by a river and on the other side of the river was a very dense forest. In the blink of an eye, I was on the other side of the river and Jesus was right next to me. He invited me to walk with Him into the woods. As we walked a small shack or hut appeared before us. It was built on the side of a tree. It looked to be completely made of gold. We climbed inside, and it was just like a small house with a main room and a kitchen.

As we spent time together, I baked Him a chocolate cake. We laughed and talked for what seemed like hours. As I came out of the vision I realized it had only been maybe 20 minutes. The Lord spoke to my heart in that moment and said He loves spending time with His children.

Also, He revealed that just as He and I spend time in our secret place, He loves to spend time in the secret place with each of His children. Each adventure with Him is a grand and different adventure. Many times I have gone back to that forest and spent time with the Lord, and many times the adventure just continued from where we last left off.

Dreams, visions, and encounters are all part of our glorious relationship with Him. They are available to everyone, and every encounter, adventure, dream or vision is unique to each person, just as we are all unique to Him.

Begin your adventure by closing your eyes and picturing Jesus standing right in front of you. Ask Him to take you to your secret place and to take you on an adventure. Every minute I spend with Jesus, He always teaches me something new. I've received understanding about things that have caused me great dilemma. I have been healed in my encounters with Him. I have seen castles and villages. I have received gifts from Him that are a part of His calling for my life or a gift of love. He loves us so much, and He loves us so well. He longs to be with His children. So, let the adventures begin.

SO MUCH MORE TO PURITY
Katharina Krison // Mystic // Germany

God once showed me a very tall building; it was maybe 80 stories high if I had to guess. The top was in the clouds, and the Lord told me that the building was a picture of purity. He showed me a sign in the lobby that read, "sexual purity." He explained that there is so much more to purity than we know. Sexual purity was merely the lobby! It's just the beginning. God is the purity that is holiness.

"Who may ascend the mountain of the Lord? Who may stand in His holy place? The one who has clean hands and a pure heart," says Psalm 24:3-4 NIV. Jesus ascended the mountain of the Lord to make it available for all who believe. He made my hands clean and my heart pure. We get stuck in the "lobby" because we're concerned about sexual purity—not that it isn't important—but, "He remembers my sins no more (Hebrews 10:17); I am washed white as snow (Psalms 51:7)!"

The top of the building went into the clouds leading directly into the heavens. That is where we belong! Jesus died to make me righteous and to move me into the heavens. My walk with God is not a journey from floor to floor as I grow in purity. He is purity and as the mystery of knowing Him more unfolds so will my revelation of purity.

The pure in heart must have tunnel vision for their Beloved. You have it. We must stop questioning what He has answered and only seek to know Him more. Your heart desires to seek His face (Psalm 24:6).

HE LOVES TO GIVE
Jeff Collins // Mystic // United States

While I was ministering in Illinois, everyone in the room fell under the anointing of the Holy Spirit. Not wanting to be left out, I placed my hand on my own head to also receive the anointing. As I went down under the Holy Spirit, I felt my spirit release and it went into the heavenly realms. As I went up and entered the throne room of God, I felt compelled to ask for things. I said, "Father, I want more of your presence. I want more of your glory, more of your anointing, and to walk more in your power." I asked for three or four holy things, not for land or money. But suddenly I felt shame come over me, "Oh Lord, I am sorry. It seems as if every time I am before you I am asking for something. Don't you feel used?" And with loving thunder He replied, "I cannot feel used for I came to give."

Then He put up a screen in front of me and flashed Scriptures on the screen. As He did this, He underlined parts of Scripture and a light of His revelation would come to me. The first Scripture He placed on the screen was John 3:16, "For God so loved the world, that he gave His only Son, that whosoever believes in Him would not perish but have everlasting life." I saw Him underline two words: He gave. The moment He underlined these two words, I was reminded of teachings that I had grown up with in the Charismatic Movement about love.

They talked about *agape* being the highest form of love and *eros* as one of the lowest forms. Another teaching talked about Paul reaching into classical Greek to try to define the sacrificial love of God. Beloved, these definitions do not begin to scratch the surface of defining the love of God. He gave!

The next scripture that flashed on the screen was one I had to look up later. He knows His word better than we do. It said, "If you then being evil know how to give good gifts to our children, how much more shall your Heavenly Father give to those who ask the Holy Spirit (Luke 11:13)." He underlined the first part: if you then being evil. I understood in that moment how twisted we are in our human nature that we feel used if people keep asking us for something, but God cannot feel that way. Then He underlined: how much more. I began to understand the unlimited resources that God has for us. There are entire warehouses filled with all kind of things appropriated for us. Some have seen body parts restored and creative miracles. Some have seen other kinds of resources. There are all kinds of things stored up in the heavenly realms for us. All we have to do is ask and receive.

The third scripture highlighted was one in Luke which says, "He Himself is kind to ungrateful and evil men." His kindness is not limited to those who claim His name. He doesn't just love, but He is love and love is always reaching. Love is always going out. It does not matter how many times it is rejected, it always seek to reach.

The last scripture the He flashed on the screen was, "Up to this time you have asked me nothing. Ask that you may receive, that your joy might be made full (John 16:24)." I understood at that moment. I felt somewhat like what Solomon may have felt when God gave him permission to ask for anything; for nothing is impossible for God. I then began to ask for things that God had on His heart, and I began to ask without shame.

A FATHER'S EMBRACE
David Morris // Mystic // United Kingdom

As I lay on the floor crying like a baby and wondering what I was doing, I saw two hands come down and pick me up. As I watched, the hands picked me up, and I was in the loving arms of my mother and father. There was a lot of light and only smiles. I watched as they simply held me and loved me. It felt amazing. Coming out of that, I just felt different. It is still hard to describe, but I felt like I did five years earlier after I apologized to God for the first time. My head was clear, all I could feel was peace, and I was crazy loved!

There was a huge shift in my walk with God from that moment forward. A great peace descended upon me that drove me deep into God's presence. He became my life source, and knowing Him was the only thing that gave me life (John 17:3). God moved more and more powerfully through me. I walked in more wisdom and more freedom, but still nothing has compared to just knowing Him.

That encounter restored me to the tree of life, a place of pure connection to God and utter dependence on my Father as a child. I became free of judgments and mindsets that I'd picked up during my life. As I grew in God, I began to see that so much of my Christian life and actions were based on my judgments or finite beliefs that weren't alive in an infinite God. Though it may have been knowledge about God that I knew to be true, it didn't come from a living relationship with Him. That knowledge was external to the living reality now within me. God showed me that Jesus didn't just pay for us to mirror His ministry. He didn't just pay for us to walk in greater things than He did, but He paid for us to have the same relationship and walk in the same way with His father as He did and still does!

This revelation propelled me to seek to do only what God is doing, as Jesus did (John 5:19). Why would I do anything else? There may be other "good" things to do, or we could try and do the "right" things, but these would come from a place of separation from God. Jesus and His Father were one (John 10:30), and Jesus died that we may be one with them as they are one (John 17:21). So now I walk in connection with God, knowing Him and His love. Doing what He is doing has become my greatest adventure!

JESUS IN ME
Katharina Krison // Mystic // Germany

As I sat in a coffee shop in Chico, California, God was moving in and around me like I'd never experienced before. I felt completely high! I could barely move or at least didn't care enough to. I was just completely absorbed by His love. Then I saw Him. There was so much light coming from His smile alone that I couldn't look anywhere else. In His smile was everything. It was pure love, so bright. His lips were made of light. I couldn't look away. He prompted me to look through Him. Looking through Him, I saw my surroundings and the other people in the coffee shop. I could only see them through Him and His love. I could see Him with every person, and with every person I saw more of Him.

"it was funny to realize that the more people there were in the room, the more Jesus there would be in any given room"

As an introvert, it was funny to realize that the more people there were in the room, the more Jesus there would be in any given room. We are invited to see as He sees and love as He loves. He genuinely enjoys spending time with us in every moment. He was so lovingly excited to stand with the girl about to order her coffee, just as much as He was with the man in the corner with headphones on. Ephesians 1:4 says, "For He chose us in Him before the creation of the world to be holy and blameless in his sight."

God has loved us since the beginning of time. God loved us before we even knew Him. Now as his new creations, we get to love as He loves, and there is no separation! As Jesus did, we also can do what the Father is doing and say what the Father is saying, for, "as He is in this world, so also are we (1 John 4:17)." The purity pouring out of His mouth is the same purity we have been restored to. Wow! We are surrounded by love and the light of Christ at all times. As believers, we have stepped into that light and see as He sees through and from love. Jesus is my ability to see and He has opened my eyes to love! I realized this means that love is effortless and constantly surrounding me. He is our eyes to see!

WE ASK, HE ANSWERS
Sheldon Watrous // Mystic // United States

I come from a long history of pastors and a rich heritage in the Lord, so it's never really been a question for me of whether He is real. The question has been: what does it look like to walk daily with this knowledge? The encounter I had with the Lord that really helped me understand how near He truly was took place several years ago during a Jason Westerfield conference. The conference was only supposed to last one week, but God began showing up in a powerful way, so it ended up going for three to four weeks instead.

One night during the conference I was walking outside and asking God: why did You choose this place? Right as I asked Him the question I went into a vision. In the vision, my church, which is 336 years old, started transforming right before my eyes. The concrete turned into brick and the electric lights became candlelit. The church went back in time, and He began to show me a group of about twenty people just praying for God to come. You could feel the compassion, the desire and hunger. When I came out of the vision I felt the Lord say, "I am not just doing this because you wanted me to do this but because there has been a legacy of people wanting and praying for this for a long time." We were literally experiencing the fulfillment of an inheritance that was fought for centuries before I was even born.

There's an understanding that we are fighting for something. But, more than that, there have been generations of people before us that have been fighting for it much longer than we have. A practical, Biblical example of this would be David. He had a vision for a temple that would house the presence of the

Lord, where individuals would minister to their God all day every day, but the fruition of his dream ended up coming through Solomon. The other beautiful thing about this was that when I asked a question, He actually answered it. When we think of the word "mystic," we think of something weird and out there, like an individual who lays on the ground for hours. That happens, but it's not very common. Mysticism is about walking daily in communion with God, and when He shows up, let Him.

Listen to Audio

NEW CREATION REALITY
Hannah F. // Mystic // Switzerland

After an evening of shopping with my roommate, we parked the car in our driveway and began to chat about life. We decided to pray together before going inside the house. After a few minutes of praying for a specific situation, the presence of God came in the car quite strongly. As we sat there enjoying the Lord, I started to have a weird sensation. I knew I was sitting in the passenger seat, but I couldn't actually feel the seat beneath me anymore. I started to see a vision. It was so clear and vivid that I felt like it was actually happening, and I was in the middle of it.

I saw myself kneeling on the floor of a big warehouse room, and I was bleeding. It all seemed a bit eerie and weird to me. Then suddenly, something like a shadow was lifted off of me, and all that was left of me was a clean, pure spirit. I began to move around in the vision, and I realized that I had no edge to me. My spirit could move freely and even material wasn't an obstacle for it. I could move through the wall of the room smoothly. I looked around in the room, and when I looked behind me, I could see other shadows like the one that was lifted off me. They were hung up on the wall and they had a dirty, demonic sense to them.

At that point, I knew in my heart that I had received a revelation of what it meant to be a new creation. The old nature was taken off of me and a new one was given. The shadows on the wall were other people's "old natures." I already believed that I was new in Christ, but this experience gave me a real heart knowledge of what that meant.

During this encounter, every time my roomate would talk to me it sounded as if she was far away from me, even though she was right beside me. The

Josh Garrels CD that was playing in the background seemed to be playing in the distance, even though I was right by the speaker.

After the encounter faded, I attempted to walk inside my house but was extremely intoxicated with the presence of God. Basically, I made it to my bed and laughed for about an hour. For the next 10 days I was almost in a constant state of complete drunkness. From that point on, I literally felt new. It felt like my spirit was crowned after the shadow was lifted off. It became easy for me to speak new creation identity into peoples' lives at a heart level. I also felt more myself than ever before. When I looked in the mirror the next morning, I suddenly liked myself a lot more and I began to feel comfortable in my own skin. Yay, God!

ENCOUNTER ME
Jason Chin // Mystic // United States

I'm a single father raising my kids, but this particular summer they went to their mother's house in Oregon. Having all this extra time I began asking God what I should do for my summer job. I grew up on a farm so I'd worked since I was 14 years old, pretty much every day of my life. But this time the Lord spoke to my heart, "Jason, I want to be your summer job." I asked Him what He meant, and He showed me a timecard with a number of hours on it. He wanted me to spend time daily, literally 5 days a week, in my room with Him.

After the kids went off to their mom's house, I was really excited to start this journey with the Lord. The first day I felt like a little kid getting out my timecard to clock in. All I know is that I prayed as long as I could, I worshiped as long as I could, and I soaked as long as I could. When I looked at the clock barely any time had passed. I tried speaking in tongues and then would look at the clock again to see only 5 minutes had passed by. I felt like a caged animal, literally about to have a panic attack because it hit me how much time I committed to doing this. It was only the first day, and I was already bored and going crazy!

For two days I did this. It felt like I was doing one of those physical, Tough-Mudder challenges in my room. Then the third or fourth day when I woke up, I felt something crazy different in my room. It reminded me of the feeling you get when you know someone is watching you, but you can't see them. I woke up with this awareness that something was in my room! It was incredible because I could literally feel the atmosphere was different. When I looked off to the right, I knew that the Holy Spirit was there. Then I heard the Holy Spirit say, "Lay back down."

As soon as I lay down, waves of His Presence started washing over me. It felt like tingling waves were shooting from toe to head and head to toe, like electricity. It was tangible love over my entire body, which just got stronger and stronger. Wave after wave began washing over me, almost in this euphoric way. With each pass it kept going deeper into me. I remember lying on my bed crying, feeling so much love and so much pleasure all at the same time. When it finally lifted, as if it was waning, I remember getting up and looking at my clock and three hours had gone by. I couldn't believe it! It felt like maybe a half an hour had passed. It was truly an "awe-inspiring" moment.

So I got up, had something to eat, and went back to my room to worship. The same Presence came back and again hours went by so quickly. I remember thinking, "Eight hours is not going to be enough time in my room!" It completely changed from me barely surviving 30 minutes to 8 hours being too little time.

When I would go out and pray for people on the streets, there was an increase, even with words of knowledge—everything was just easier! I would know things about people as I walked up to them, when before I would have to try hard to get a word of knowledge. Now when I walked up to a group of people, I could see what the problem was before I even got there. Also, people noticed God's Presence on me before I even talked to them. They would say, "When you walked up, I got chills all over me." It was the Presence going with me. But even then, the whole time I was on the streets, I would be longing to go back to my bedroom.

I would literally come into my house, shut the door and run down my hallway just to get back to my room. God would be there! My room would be electrified—I just couldn't get enough time in my room! Then other things started to happen—wind started blowing in my room, but I'm also a realist. Since I wouldn't call lint an angel feather, I wanted to make sure the wind I was feeling was legitimate. So I got duck tape and taped all my windows, my door and anywhere I thought wind might be able to come through. I sat there and said, "Holy Spirit, I love you so much. I am just so thankful for Your Presence." Then a wind or a breeze would start blowing in my room. Flashes of light started appearing in my room. So I turned off the lights and boarded up my windows with cardboard because I just wanted to make sure it was real; I wanted an authentic encounter.

I looked like the neighborhood drug dealer because I would spend hours in my house with my windows boarded up and duck tape on areas that a breeze could slip through! There was no way that light or wind could come in. Every time I would say, "Jesus I love you so much," I saw flashes of light and felt wind blowing.

Then other things started happening. I would leave my room, and when I would come back there would be candy wrappers on my bed and floor. It didn't make sense! Nobody else was home. God would literally put candy wrappers on my bed, and it was mostly strawberry Starburst wrappers everywhere. So I would clean my bed off before I left. When I came back, wrappers would be everywhere again, even in my hand. I would be sitting there, and a strawberry Starburst wrapper would materialize in my hand! My room is still my favorite place on earth!

God also started taking me places in my spirit. One time a radio appeared in my room where the channel would change and the stock market would start playing as clearly as any conversation. A man would come on and start talking about the housing market and retirement trusts, and I would just sit there and write it all down. Then I would hear the radio change again, and it would change to the Spanish channel and I heard a family talking.

Another time I was sitting in my room, and a Todd Bentley podcast started playing. He was talking about how God would take him on these translations, "When God would take me up in the spirit, I would always go out through the same doorway—which is the Revelations 4 door and also the John 10:9 door. This door is Jesus and each time I go a little bit further and I can stay out a little bit longer." When I personally tried this, I would go into my room and lay down. The second I lay down everything would go black, and I would end up in a different realm. I was fully conscious and aware, but I didn't know where my body was. I was off in another dimension. Then a white light would appear in the distance. As it came closer, it ended up being the silhouette of a bright white person, but I could never see His face because He was so radiant white. It was Jesus.

When He came up to me, it was so profound. I started having interesting encounters. I used to have a problem with the idea of seeing Jesus in a romantic way, as my husband like it says in Scripture. I'm a guy, and He's a guy. It was just hard to engage with Him in any other way than as a brother. So one of my friends would constantly pray for me to receive the revelation of being His bride, like in Song of Solomon.

In this encounter, Jesus came up to me and stepped inside me. It was the most euphoric thing I have ever experienced in my life. It was better than any pleasure the world has to offer. With all of my heart, I can tell you that there is nothing this earth has to offer better than Him! In that moment, Jesus became my everything. In that moment, He ruined me for anything but Him. I am ruined now. There is nothing you can offer me that would even come close. I know it because I experienced it. I came out of that encounter so in love. I was like the guy that just got a girlfriend! Puppy love!

Everywhere I went I found myself saying, "Have you heard about Jesus?! Have you heard about Jesus?!" I just couldn't shut up about Jesus.

Everywhere I went I was captivated with this romantic type of love. I was in love! It felt like my feet weren't even touching the ground. And I still haven't gotten over Him yet. That moment marked me. That summer after first year was the defining time of my life. Those experiences, the revelation, the friendship and taking time to get away with Him changed me. All the success I've had and anything that I do now, I know it stems from that secret place and that time that I spent behind closed doors with only Him. It honestly has fulfilled me, even if nothing else happens in any sort of public eye… I would be the most satisfied human being alive.

Lovesaysgo.com

St. Francis
(ca. 1181 – 1226)

"Preach the Gospel at all times and when necessary use words."

"I have been all things unholy. If God can work through me, he can work through anyone."

Born around 1181, Francis was known for following all that Jesus said and did. He embraced a life of prayer and sought to empty himself of all worldliness. He sought to become one with Christ. One event in particular showed his identification with Christ in 1224. He became the first recorded person to ever receive the stigmata. Francis had embarked on a journey to Mt. La Verna for a forty-day fast. One morning while he was praying, Francis had a vision of a six-winged Seraphim standing above him with its hands stretched out and its feet nailed to a cross. Francis could barely comprehend the beauty of the Seraphim, which gazed at him with kindness.

At the same time, Francis was also filled with sorrow at the sight of this beautiful creature being nailed to the cross. After this vision, while pondering what it meant, the signs of the nails began to appear in Francis' own hands and feet. His hands and feet appeared as if they had been pierced in the middle by nails, with nail heads showing on the inner side of the hands. On both his hands and feet, the flesh at the top of the nails was raised. His right side also bore a scar, as though it had been pierced by a spear. This wound frequently dropped blood, which would stain his clothing. St. Francis' vision blurred the lines between the spiritual and the physical, with the two merging as if they were never meant to be apart.

Daniel
(bc. 7th – 6th Century)

Numbers 12:6 *"Hear now my words. If there is a prophet among you, I Yahweh will make myself known to him in a vision. I will speak with him in a dream."*

Not a great deal is known about Daniel. The Scriptures suggest that he may have been from noble descent (Daniel 1:3). He was taken as a captive to Babylon during King Jehoiakim's reign (Daniel 1:2). Daniel had a long career in captivity under several oppressive regimes, possibly spanning 70 years. From a young age Daniel exhibited gifts generally associated with mystics. For example, he had vivid dreams and visions and interpreted dreams as well as angelic visitations.

"In my vision at night I looked, and there before me was one like the son of man, coming with the clouds of heaven."

In Daniel 7:13 -14 he described one of his visions, "In my vision at night I looked, and there before me was one like the son of man, coming with the clouds of heaven. He approached the Ancient of Days and was led into his presence. He was given authority, glory and sovereign power; all peoples, nations and men of every language worshiped him. His dominion is an everlasting dominion that will not pass away, and his kingdom will be one that will never be destroyed."

There is also a marvelous account of Daniel meeting the angel Gabriel in Daniel 8:15-18,"While I, Daniel was watching the vision and trying to understand it, there before me stood one who looked like a man. And I heard a man's voice from the banks of Ulai calling, and he called out and said, 'Gabriel, tell this man the meaning of the vision.'

The book of Daniel serves as an apocalyptic book in the Bible. The recordings of this mystic's spectacular visions provided not only the people of Israel, but also all mankind, insight into God's plans for the Messiah and the end times.

CONCLUSION

Tim Oliver // MDCM Anthology Team // New Zealand

It is possible, and we are of course hopeful, that the encounters and experiences described in this book have given you a sense of awe and wonder at what is possible and available to you as a Spirit-filled believer. It is equally possible that the testimonies of our modern day mystics have left you feeling somewhat outside your comfort zone, as you now ask yourself, "Is this actually real or are these 'mystics' simply telling fantastic tales?"

We will simply say this. God cannot be put in a box. And in order for us to grow, it is crucial that we do not try to limit God to what we have personally already experienced. You do not need to understand everything contained in this book. In fact, our natural reasoning and human minds can be a stumbling block to receiving and understanding the Kingdom. Bill Johnson puts it simply when he says, "Not understanding is OK. Restricting our spiritual life to what we understand is not."[1] Therefore it is crucial to remember this: if you greatly desire spiritual growth, you must be willing to accept matters of the Kingdom that you do not understand with childlike faith.

It is a privilege to be able to share the personal experiences and revelations of the mystics contained in this book. And when we say "share" we do not simply mean "to read about." What you have read is both an invitation and an impartation to experience these same kinds of mystical encounters for yourself. Remember, God is no respecter of persons, and He longs to encounter you. If you desire more of God's Kingdom, you simply need to ask Him and receive in faith.

We bless you on your journey, and we pray that as you seek and ask God to reveal more of Himself, that you will experience amazing personal union with God. We also declare over you Ephesians 3:20—that God will do immeasurably more for you than you ever dreamed or imagined was possible!

Union with God is more than terminology or another formula to get something we want. Union with God is a reality that brings Him into every part of our every day life. It is the greatest romance; it is the greatest adventure one can ever take. If you're up to it, let Him pursue you and you Him. Let this romance be a lifestyle, not just the next fun fling.

1   Bill Johnson, *'Dreaming with God - Secrets to Redesigning Your World Through God's Creative Flow,'* page 56.   Destiny Images Publishers, Inc, released 2006.

BIBLICAL ENCOUNTERS DIRECTORY

From the very beginning of the Bible to its end, there are many Biblical characters who had ecstatic encounters and revelations with God. This list is not comprehensive but merely a guide to help better characterize how God interacted with mankind. By looking at past encounters we hope to expand our expectations of how God desires to interact with us today.

Angelic Visitations

There are 209 occurrences of the word "Angel" in the Bible, while the word "Angels" appears 99 times.

Genesis 21:17	Angel delivers a message to Hagar.
Genesis 32.22-31	Angel wrestles with Jacob.
Judges 6:12	Angel appears to Gideon, prophesies over him and gives him instruction.
1 Kings 19:5	Angel prepares Elijah for Mt. Horeb.
Daniel 6:22	Angel shuts the mouths of lions.
Daniel 9:10	The archangel Gabriel tells Daniel that the Messiah would come in the flesh.
Daniel 10:1	Daniel has an intense angelic encounter after a 21-day fast.
Joshua 5:13	Angel trains Joshua for the Promised Land.

Matthew 1:20	Angel appears to Joseph in a dream.
Matthew 2:13	Angel appears to Joseph in a dream a second time.
Matthew 4:11	Angels come to minister to Jesus.
Matthew 28:2	Reaction of the guards by Jesus' tomb at the angel's appearance.
Luke 1:11,	Angel appears to Zachariah while in the temple.
Luke 1:28	Angel appears to Mary.
Luke 2:9	Host of angels appear to shepherds in the Fields.
John 20:12	Mary Magdalene talks with an angel.
Acts 8:26	Angel of The Lord appears to Philip.
Acts10:3	Angel appears to Cornelius.

Dance

"Dance" is mentioned 18 times in the Bible with several verses even instructing us to dance.

2 Samuel 6:14-23	David dances undignified in just a linen ephod.
Psalms 149:3	"Let them praise his name in the dance!"
Luke 6:23	Jesus said, "Be glad at such a time, and dance for joy…"

Dreams

Dreams are discussed 82 times in the Bible, while the word "dreams" appears 34 times.

Genesis 20	The Lord speaks to Abimelech in a dream warning him not to take Sarah as his wife.
Genesis 28:10 - 17	Jacob has a dream about a stairway to heaven. God talks to him and reveals His plans for the coming generation.
Genesis 31:10	Angel speaks to Jacob in a dream.
Genesis 37:5	God gives Joseph an idea of his calling.
Genesis 40:5	The cupbearer and the baker of the king have a dream and Joseph gaves the interpretation.
1 Kings 3:5	God appears to Solomon in a dream and asks what he desires.
Daniel 2:1	Nebuchadnezzar has a dream, and Daniel gives the interpretation.
Matthew 1:20	Joseph receives instructions from an angel in his dream about Jesus being conceived by the Holy Spirit.
Matthew 2:12	Joseph receives instructions in a dream to escape to Egypt.
Matthew 2:19,22	Joseph is told that Herod is dead by an angel in a dream.
Matthew 27:19	Pilate's wife warns him after suffering in her dreams.

Heaven

Heaven in one form or another is mentioned 653 times, while "Heavens" is mentioned 548 times in the Bible.

2 Kings 6:15-17	Elisha and his servant see horses and chariots of fire and a heavenly army to protect them.
2 Chronicles 18:18	Micaiah sees the Lord sitting upon His Throne.
Isaiah 6:1	Isaiah sees the Lord on His throne and His train fills the temple.
Ezekiel 1:1	The heavens opened and he sees visions of God. This continues to be the theme throughout the entire book of Ezekiel where he even sees different types of angels.
Ezekiel 10:1	Ezekial sees a throne with cherubim.
Daniel 7:9	Daniel sees the throne with the Ancient of Days on it.
Mark 1:9-11	Jesus sees the heavens open and a voice speaks to Him from the heavens.
Acts 7:55	Stephen looks up to heaven and sees the glory of the God and Jesus standing at the right hand of God.
2 Corinthians 12:2	Paul knows a man (likely himself) that is caught up to the third heaven and hears "inexpressible words."
Revelation 4:1-11	John sees the throne of God and the many elders surrounding the throne.
Revelations 21	John talks of the New Heaven and Earth.

Miracles

While miracles are recorded all throughout the Bible, the actual word "miracle" occurs only 15 times, and the word "miracles" is mentioned 65 times in the Bible.

Exodus 3:2	Moses sees the famous burning bush.
Exodus 7 – 11	10 Plagues against Egypt
Exodus 13:21	The presence of the Lord manifests by day in a pillar of cloud and by night in a pillar of fire.
Exodus 24:15	Moses has a 40-day encounter on Mount Sinai. Mount Sinai looks like a devouring fire and everyone can see the cloud of God's presence.
Exodus 33:11	God speaks to Moses "face to face—like a friend."
Exodus 33.18	Moses has another encounter with the glory of God.
Exodus 34:28	Moses has another 40 day encounter, and God gives him the New Stone Tablets. When he comes down from the mountain, his face is radiant so much that he has to cover it!
Numbers 11:25	The Lord comes down in a cloud.
Numbers 12:5	The Lord comes down in a pillar of cloud.
Numbers 20:6	The glory of God appears, and Moses falls down on his face.
Numbers 22.28	A donkey talks with Balaam.
Deuteronomy 31:15	An angel moves the pillar of cloud from the front to the top of the Hebrew congregation.
1 Samuel 19:23	Saul has another ecstatic encounter.

1 Samuel 19:19	Everyone who comes close to David and Samuel has ecstatic encounters.
1 King 8:8	The glory of God is so strong that the priests can't do their work in the temple.
1 Kings 19	Elijah encounters God at Mount Horeb.
2 Kings 6:6	Elisha and the floating iron
Judges 15:14	Samson receives supernatural strength.
Judges 14:6	The Spirit of God comes upon Samson, and he kills a lion.
1 Samuel 5:1	The Philistines are cursed when they steal the Ark of the Covenant.
Isaiah 38:8	God makes the shadow of the sun move 10 steps backwards as a sign to Hezekiah that his life will be extended another 15 years.

Miracles by Jesus

Matthew 8:1-4	Cleanses a man with leprosy
Matthew 8:5-13	Heals the Centurion's servant
Matthew 8:14-15	Heals Peter's Mother-in-Law
Matthew 8:16-17	Heals many sick
Matthew 8:23-27	Calms a storm
Matthew 8:28-33	Casts demons out of man and sends them into a herd of pigs
Matthew 9:1-8	Heals a paralytic man
Matthew 9:18, 23-26	Raises Jairus' daughter from the dead
Matthew 9:20-22	Heals women in a crowd
Matthew 9:27-31	Heals two men that were blind
Matthew 9:32-34	Heals a man that was mute
Matthew 12:9-14	Heals a man's withered hand
Matthew 12:22-23	Heals a blind, mute demoniac
Matthew 14:13-21	Feeds 5,000
Matthew 14;22-33	Walks on water

Matthew 14:34-36	Heals many sick in Gennesaret
Matthew 15:21-28	Casts out a demon from a Gentile's daughter
Matthew 15:32-39	Feeds 4,000
Matthew 17:14-20	Heals a boy with a demon
Matthew 17:24-27	Gets temple tax from a fish's mouth
Matthew 20:29-34	Heals blind Bartimaeus
Matthew 21:18-22	Withers a fig tree
Mark 1:21-27	Casts out an evil spirit
Mark 7:31-37	Heals a deaf and mute man
Mark 8:22-26	Heals a blind man
Luke 5:1-11	Miraculous catch of fish
Luke 7:11-17	Heals a widow's son
Luke 13:10-17	Heals a crippled woman
Luke 14:1-6	Heals a man with dropsy
Luke 17:11-19	Cleanses ten lepers
Luke 22:50-51	Heals the soldier's ear that was cut off by Peter
John 2:1-11	Turns water into wine
John 4:43-54	Heals an official's son
John 5:1-15	Heals an invalid at Bethesda
John 9:1-12	Heals a man who was born blind
John 11:1-45	Raises Lazarus from the dead
John 21:4-11	Miraculous catch of fish

Miracles by Peter

Acts 3:7	Heals a lame man
Acts 5:15	His shadow cures the sick
Acts 9:40	Dorcas is brought back to life

Miracles by Paul

Acts 13:11	Elymas is blinded

Acts 14:1	Lame man is cured
Acts 16:18	Casts out spirit of divination from a girl
Acts 20:10	Eutychus is restored to life
Acts 28:5	Viper bite doesn't kill Paul

Miracle by Stephen

Acts 6:8	Full of grace and power performed many signs

Miracle by Philip

Acts 8:6-13	Is recognized by the crowds for his many signs

Transportations

Although the exact words "transportations" or "translations" are not directly used in the Bible, the occurrence of such phenomenon is recorded.

Genesis 5:24	Enoch transport into eternity.
1 Kings 18:44-46	Elijah outruns a chariot.
2 Kings 2:11	Elijah transports into eternity by a whirlwind.
Ezekiel 3:12-16	Ezekial transports to the river of Chebar for 7 days.
Ezekiel 8:3	Ezekiel is lifted into the sky and is transported to the North Gate of Jerusalem.
Ezekiel 37	The Holy Spirit takes Ezekiel to another place, and Ezekiel prophesies over dry bones which come back to life.

Acts 8:26-40	The Spirit suddenly takes Philip away after he baptizes the eunuch, and the eunuch does not see him again. Philip then appears at Azotus.

Trances

The word "trance" is mentioned 7 times in the Bible.

Numbers 24:4	Balaam falls into a trance with his eyes open (King James Bible & many other translations).
Numbers 24:16	Balaam falls into a trance with his eyes open (King James Bible).
Daniel 8:18	Daniel falls into a trance-like sleep (NET Bible & Young's Literal Translation).
Daniel 10:9	As Daniel hears the words, he falls to the ground in a trance-like sleep (NET Bible & Young's Literal Translation).
Acts 10:10	Peter falls into a trance and has a vision.
Acts 11:5	Peter retells the story of falling into a trance and having a vision.
Acts 22:17	Paul's account of a trance-like experience while in Jerusalem.

Visions

There are 106 occurrences of the word "vision" in the Bible and 43 appearances of the word "visions."

Genesis 15/17/18	Abraham has a vision and makes a covenant with God.
1 Samuel 3:15	Samuel has a vision that he is afraid to share it with Eli.
2 Samuel 7:17	Nathan speaks to David out of the visions he has.
1 Kings 3:5	The Lord comes to Solomon in a vision.
2 King 6	God permits Elisha to see the heavenly host of the Lord like horses and fire chariots.
Daniel 4:5	Daniel has visions that terrify him.
Daniel 7:9	Daniel has a very detailed vision about Jesus and the glory of God.
Isaiah 6:5	Commission of Isaiah in a heavenly vision
Ezekiel 1-3	Ezekiel describes "heaven opened" which he saw in a vision and was given instructions for Israel,
Ezekiel 11:22	Ezekiel has a powerful vision of God's glory.
Obadiah 1:1	Obadiah revealing the vision from the Lord.
Zechariah 3	Zachariah stands before the Lord and Satan accuses him but God covers him.
Acts 9:10 -16	The Lord appears to Ananias in a vision.
Acts18:9	The Lord speaks to Paul in a vision.
Hebrews 12:21	"And the vision was so overpowering that even Moses said, I am shaking and full of fear."
2 Corinthians 12:1	Paul refers to his visions and revelations.
Revelations 1-22	John's vision of the end times and heaven.

MDCM ANTHOLOGY TEAM

MDCM: *Modern Day Christian Mystics*

Written and Compiled by
Miscellaneous Mystics, Denise Allen, Lauren Detombe, Kalina Georgieva, Tim Oliver, Daniel Ruggaber, Nick Wallace

Edited by Stefanie Overstreet, Hailley Jo Holcombe
Illustrations by Daniel Ruggaber, Nick Wallace
Website Design by Nick Wallace
Book Formatting by Nick Wallace
Team Leader Nick Wallace

Left to Right: Denise Allen, Tim Oliver, Kalina Georgieva, Nick Wallace, Lauren DeTombe, and Daniel Ruggaber

www.ingramcontent.com/pod-product-compliance
Lightning Source LLC
LaVergne TN
LVHW052025080426
835513LV00018B/2172